FOLENS IDEAS BANK MINIBEASTS

Malcolm Dixon
Karen Smith

Contents

How to use this book	2	Caterpillars	22
Introduction	3	Butterflies	24
		Ants	26
Looking for minibeasts	4	Earwigs	28
Land study	6	Aphids	30
Freshwater study	8	Beetles	32
Snails 1	10	Ladybirds	34
Snails 2	12	Spiders	36
Slugs	14	Centipedes	38
Earthworms	16	Millipedes	40
Woodlice	18	Classifying minibeasts	42
Stick insects	20	Identifying minibeasts	44

How to use this book

Ideas Bank books provide ready to use, practical, photocopiable activity pages for children, **plus** a wealth of ideas for extension and development.

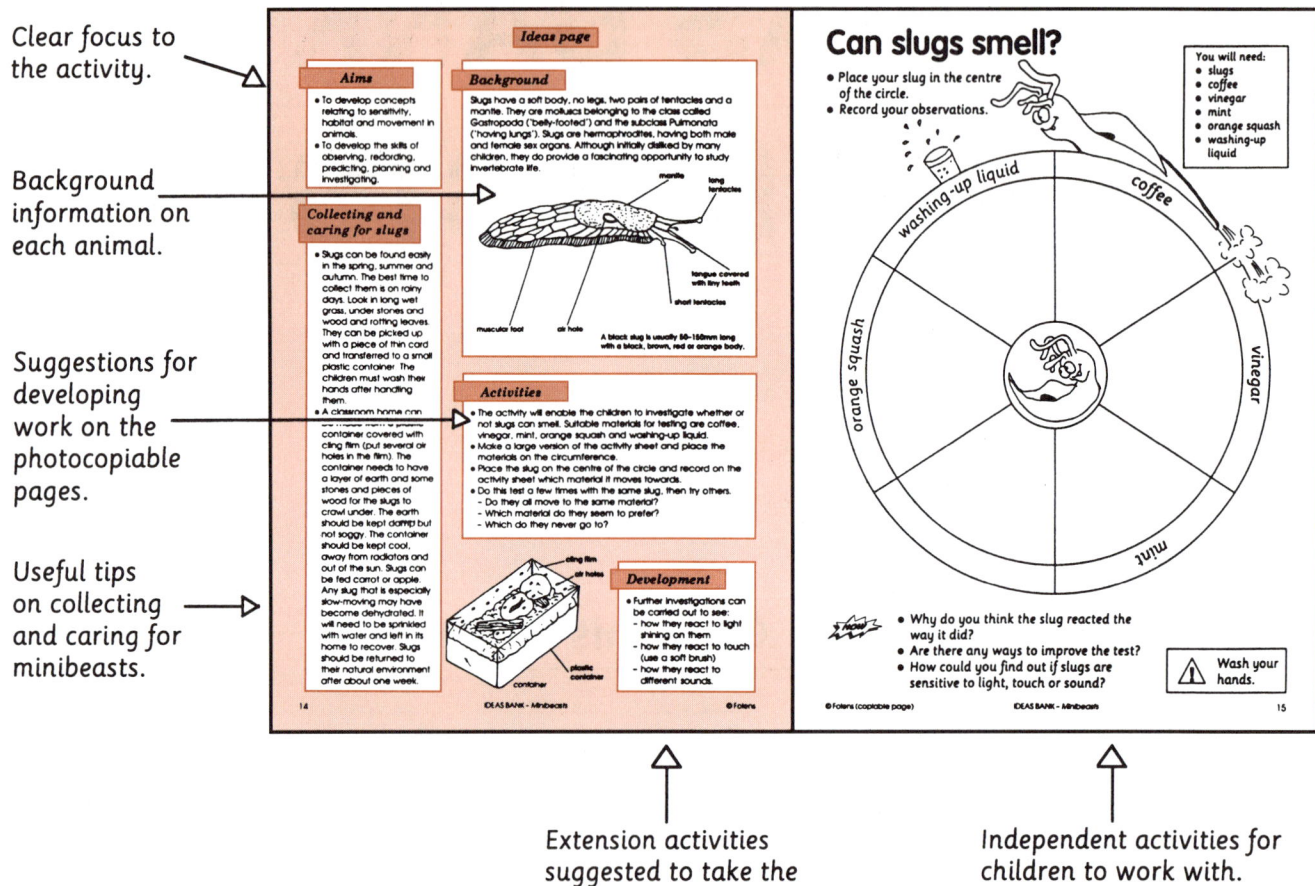

- Clear focus to the activity.
- Background information on each animal.
- Suggestions for developing work on the photocopiable pages.
- Useful tips on collecting and caring for minibeasts.
- Extension activities suggested to take the work one stage further.
- Independent activities for children to work with.

Folens allows photocopying of pages marked 'copiable page' for educational use, providing that this use is within the confines of the purchasing institution. Copiable pages should not be declared in any return in respect of any photocopying licence.

Folens books are protected by international copyright laws. All rights are reserved. The copyright of all materials in this book, except where otherwise stated, remains the property of the publisher and author(s). No part of this publication may be reproduced, stored in a retrieval system, or transmitted, in any form or by any means, for whatever purpose, without the written permission of Folens Limited.

This resource may be used in a variety of ways. However, it is not intended that teachers or children should write directly into the book itself. Malcolm Dixon and Karen Smith hereby assert their moral rights to be identified as the authors of this work in accordance with the Copyright, Designs and Patents Act 1988.

Editor: Claire Ancell
Illustrations: Teresa O'Brien
Layout artist: Patricia Hollingsworth
Cover image: Zefa
Cover design: In Touch Creative Services

© 1996 Folens Limited, on behalf of the authors.

Every effort has been made to contact copyright holders of material used in this book. If any have been overlooked, we will be pleased to make any necessary arrangements.

British Library Cataloguing in Publication Data. A catalogue record for this book is available from the British Library.

First published 1996 by Folens Limited, Dunstable and Dublin.

Folens Limited, Albert House, Apex Business Centre, Boscombe Road, Dunstable, LU5 4RL, England.

ISBN 1 85276014-1

Printed in Singapore by Craft Print

Introduction

The word 'minibeasts' refers to a variety of small animals which are all invertebrates. It is important to recognise that not all of them are insects – since insects are only a sub-group of the world of minibeasts.

This book contains easily-accessible background knowledge, ideas for activities and activity sheets for use by children. It is intended that teachers select activities to form a scheme of work for their particular class of children considering age, ability, progression and the need for differentiation. The book could also be used as a resource to 'dip into' when an interesting minibeast arrives in the classroom!

The activities are designed to develop scientific skills and important biological ideas. These ideas refer to life processes and living things and include nutrition, movement, growth, reproduction, breathing, sensitivity, variety and classification, adaptation, habitat, food chains and interdependence.

The activity sheets allow the children to indulge in the 'process' skills of science: planning and carrying out investigations, making predictions, comparing, observing, measuring, considering how to make a test fair, presenting results and drawing conclusions. The emphasis is on the importance of conservation and the encouragement of a caring attitude towards living things and their environments.

The minibeasts chosen are found easily in both urban and rural environments. Diagrams throughout the book will help with identification. Keeping and caring for minibeasts can engender both moral and spiritual development.

When teaching about minibeasts the following should be considered:
- The summer term is probably the best time since the animals are abundant and the weather is appropriate for outdoor work.
- Ensure that a selection of well-illustrated information books is available for the children to consult in the classroom.
- Do not use containers made from glass for collecting or keeping minibeasts.
- Ensure that the children wash their hands with soap before and immediately after handling minibeasts or their containers.
- Look for opportunities to use information technology in developing the topic.
- Involve the children in displaying their work in the classroom or school corridors.
- Be sympathetic to those children who are afraid of some minibeasts or find them distasteful. Some of this behaviour is learned at home from adults. Let them overcome their fears gradually as they become accustomed to minibeasts. A teacher who has genuine fears about minibeasts should seriously consider whether this topic would be better taught by a colleague.
- Children should be encouraged to generate their own questions and to plan and carry out investigations.
- Children come to the topic with their own ideas about minibeasts – sometimes called 'children's science' or 'alternative frameworks' – which may be at odds with accepted 'scientific' views. Discuss their ideas using annotated drawings, concept maps and so on, to plan a strategy to help them to revise their own ideas.

Identifying minibeasts

Page 44	Page 45	Page 46	Page 47	Page 48
butterfly	adult ground beetle	black slug	woodlouse	water boatman
caterpillar	devil's coach horse beetle	garden slug	soil centipede	pond skater
earthworm	longhorn beetle	great grey slug	stone centipede	gnat
stick insect	scarab beetle	keeled slug	black millipede	water louse
garden spider	soldier beetle	snail	flat-backed millipede	mayfly larva
house spider	spider beetle	aphids	pill millipede	stonefly larva
ladybirds	stag beetle	ant	spotted snake millipede	freshwater shrimp
	weevil	earwig	striped millipede	caddisfly larva

© Folens   IDEAS BANK – *Minibeasts*

Looking for minibeasts – Ideas page

Aims

- To introduce children to a variety of minibeasts within the environment.
- To develop an appreciation of the need to care properly for living things.
- To develop the scientific skills of observing and recording.

Preparation

Minibeasts select an environment with suitable characteristics, and land minibeasts will move from an unsuitable environment to one with optimum conditions. Looking for minibeasts is best carried out in the spring and summer when the children will be able to appreciate the great diversity of minibeasts even within a small area. Ideally, for this activity a site should be chosen that has a range of habitats, such as long grass, damp and dry areas, flowers, weeds and light and shady areas. This may be in the school grounds, a public park or in a nature reserve. A prior visit is essential.

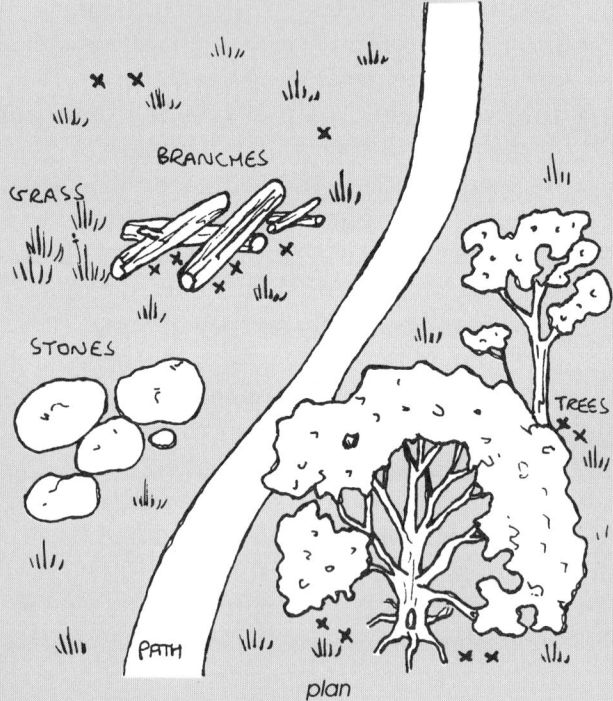

plan

Collecting and caring for minibeasts

It is important that children recognise that indiscriminate collecting of minibeasts, or damage to the environment while collecting, can cause havoc to the animal population of an area. It is useful to give them a 'collector's code':

- Search carefully and disturb the surroundings as little as possible.
- Collect a few animals at a time for study.
- Handle the animals carefully. Use spoons and damp brushes, never use fingers.

spoon and brush

- Replace stones and logs after searching underneath them.
- Never remove plants.
- Have small plastic containers to place minibeasts in.
- When collecting keep different minibeasts in separate containers.
- After a short time return minibeasts to where they were found or make suitable classroom homes for them.

Activities

- Show the children how to use the activity sheet. Introduce and discuss the 'collector's code'.
- Give them some guidance on what they are to look for, how to collect the minibeasts and how many they should collect (ideally 10–12).
- Working in a defined area, the class can be divided into groups, each of which is allocated smaller areas to explore. One member of each group should be given the task of completing the activity sheet.
- Later a whole class discussion should focus on the variety and numbers of minibeasts that were found within the chosen environment.

Development

- The identification cards (pages 44–48) may help the children with the identification of individual minibeasts. Photographs of minibeasts and information books should also be available in the classroom.

Where do minibeasts live?

You will need:
- spoon
- paintbrush
- small containers
- identification cards
- magnifier
- pencil

- On the chart below, record what you found in your search for minibeasts. Use identification cards and reference books to help you to identify them.

Minibeast	Where found	Number

- On the back of this sheet, sketch the place where you have been looking for minibeasts. Show areas that are light or shady, have long or short grass, are damp or dry, have flower beds, paths, logs, stones and so on. Mark on it where you found the minibeasts. Compare your findings with those of your friends.

 Do not eat while working with minibeasts. Keep your hands away from your face. Wash your hands afterwards.

© Folens (copiable page)   IDEAS BANK – *Minibeasts*

Land study – Ideas page

Aims

- To understand that animals can be identified and classified according to external characteristics.
- To understand that different animals are found in different habitats.
- To understand that animals are adapted to their environment.
- To use focused exploration to acquire scientific knowledge.

Background

The distribution and variety of animals in any one location is dependent on the surrounding physical conditions, for example damp/dry, light/dark, warm/cool, sheltered/open, nature of vegetation.

Collecting and caring for land minibeasts

There are three methods of collecting land animals.
- By hand. Animals that are attached to plants (on the underside of leaves and where the leaves are joined to the stem) can be removed carefully by hand. A plastic spoon or paintbrush is useful for transferring them to a plastic container.
- A pooter is more suitable for collecting small, fast moving animals. Children with breathing difficulties should not be asked to use a pooter. Wash the plastic tubing after each child has used it.
- Sweeping and beating. A large net is swept through the grass, or the grass can be shaken vigorously or beaten to dislodge any animals. They are collected in a shallow tray placed underneath the plants.

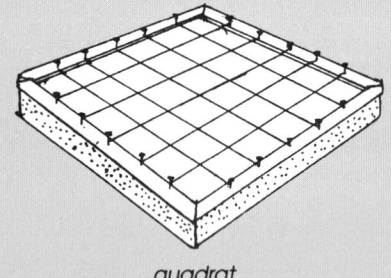
quadrat

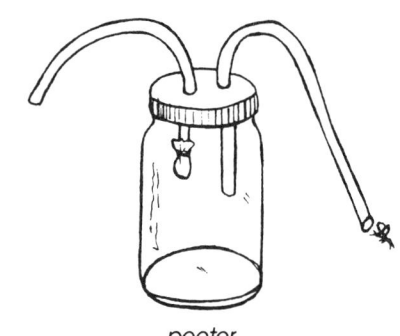
pooter

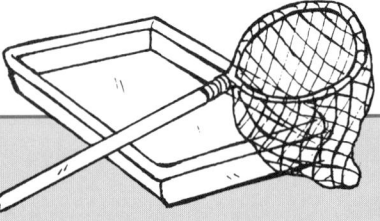
net and tray

Activities

- Find two contrasting areas to investigate, such as a mown field and an unmown one. Ask the children if there is anything special about the two habitats.
- Divide the class into groups, give each group an activity sheet and explain it to them.
- Ask them to sketch both areas on the back of the sheet then record the individual minibeasts found there. They could label the sketch with the type of vegetation: flowering/non-flowering plants; degree of shade; moisture content of the soil; rocks; leaf litter; evidence of pollution.
- Let one child from each group throw a quadrat randomly into each habitat. (A quadrat is a frame used for sampling the flora or fauna within an area. For these investigations an opened coat hanger will suffice.) The children should collect the animals in each quadrat, observe and identify them. They then record their observations on the activity sheet.
- Ideally, this procedure should be repeated three more times in order to introduce some degree of reliability/validity.

Development

- Ask the children to use information books to determine the preferable living conditions of the individual minibeasts that they have found.
- They could consider their secondary sources of information and the observed physical conditions in order to suggest reasons why different animals are located in different habitats.

What is found where?

You will need:
- quadrats
- pooter
- small transparent containers
- collecting tray
- sweep net
- paintbrush/spoon
- clipboard/pencil
- identification cards

- Find two different types of habitat, one with the grass long and the other with it mown. With the quadrat, select four different parts of each habitat and investigate each area carefully.

- Make a record of the variety and number of minibeasts found in each quadrat.

	Q1	Q2	Q3	Q4
Mown				

	Q1	Q2	Q3	Q4
Unmown				

- Use information books to find out the conditions each minibeast prefers.
- Look at your observations.
- Suggest reasons why different animals live in different habitats.

© Folens (copiable page)   IDEAS BANK – *Minibeasts*   7

Freshwater study – Ideas page

Aims

- To recognise that different animals can be found in contrasting habitats.
- To observe, measure and record the varying conditions within an environment.

Collecting and caring for freshwater minibeasts

- Running water: many of the animals found in running water are adapted to withstand currents, so look for them under stones, attached to plants and on the river bed. To collect them from under stones, place a net downstream of the stone, then lift the stone carefully. Any animals that escape may go into the net; others can be found under the stone itself. To sample the river bed, place a net downstream and kick the river floor three times to disturb the animals.
- Still water: sweep a plastic gravy strainer or a fishing net through the water. Tip the contents into a shallow container.
- Any nets used should have a very small mesh.
- Avoid transporting a mixed catch or you may return to school with one very fat carnivore in your container! Return the animals to their place of origin as soon as possible.

Background

Running water has a high oxygen content and many of the animals found there will be adapted to this. These tend to be either strong swimmers, possess some means of anchorage or have flattened bodies to offer the least resistance to the water flow. In slower moving water plants are able to take root, providing shelter for animal life such as snails and worms.

To study a specific area of freshwater, it is best to go about it in a scientific way. This is done by taking a transect, ensuring that different aspects of the environment are studied. Stretch a piece of string across the width of the water. Determine the various depths of the water by placing canes at measured intervals along the string. Mark the depth of the water on each of the canes. Remove the canes and measure the depths. Record the measurements on graph paper to give a profile of the water bed.

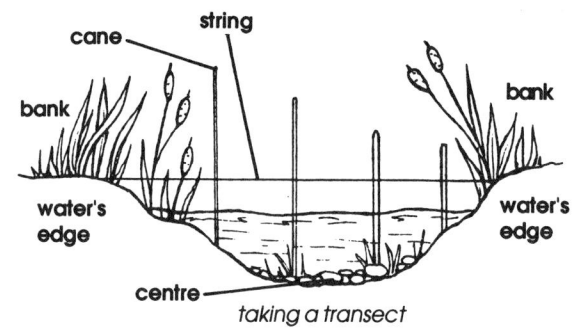

taking a transect

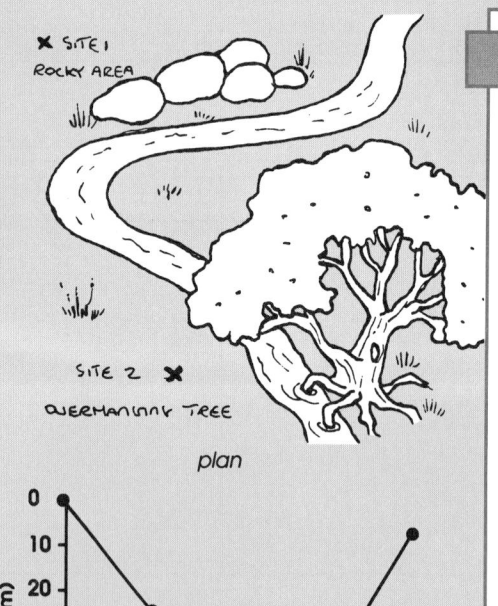

plan

transect graph

Activities

- Encourage the children to produce a plan of the area selected, showing the two sites from which they will take measurements and samples.
- They should then record the immediate surroundings for each site.
- The activity page is a record sheet that requires them to take a transect and then quantify the animals collected at each site.

Development

- Ask the children to produce observational drawings and record similarities and differences between the animals.

Freshwater study

You will need:
- net
- plastic gravy strainer
- shallow container
- containers with holes in lids
- clipboard
- pencil
- string
- canes
- tape measure

- On the back of this sheet sketch a plan of the area of freshwater you are investigating, marking two selected sites.
- Take a transect at each site and mark your measurements on the graphs below. This will give a profile of the water bed.
- Collect, identify and count the minibeasts found near the banks, the water's edge and in the centre.

Record	Near bank	Near water's edge	Centre	Far water's edge	Far bank
SITE 1 Number and type of minibeasts					
SITE 2 Number and type of minibeasts					

- Record your transect results.

- Can you suggest reasons why different animals are found in different habitats?
- How are they adapted?

 Wash your hands.

© Folens (copiable page)   IDEAS BANK – *Minibeasts*   9

Snails 1 – Ideas page

Aims

- To understand that there are life processes – movement, nutrition, respiration, sensitivity, reproduction, excretion – common to animals.
- To generate questions that can be investigated.

Activities

- Divide the children into pairs and give each pair at least one snail. Ask them to list their observations.
- Provide some food so that they can watch the feeding mechanism. Putting the snail on a small, transparent Perspex sheet will help with observing movement and feeding.
- Ask them to complete the activity sheet.
- Hold a report-back session to discuss the relevant observations and life processes.

Development

From their observations the children could go on to devise and answer their own questions, such as:
- How fast do snails move?
- What is a snail's favourite food?
- Does the length of the foot make any difference to a snail's speed?
- Does the snail move faster on rough or smooth surfaces?
- Can the snail see in the dark?

Background

Snails are molluscs, belonging to the class Gastropoda, which means 'belly footed'.

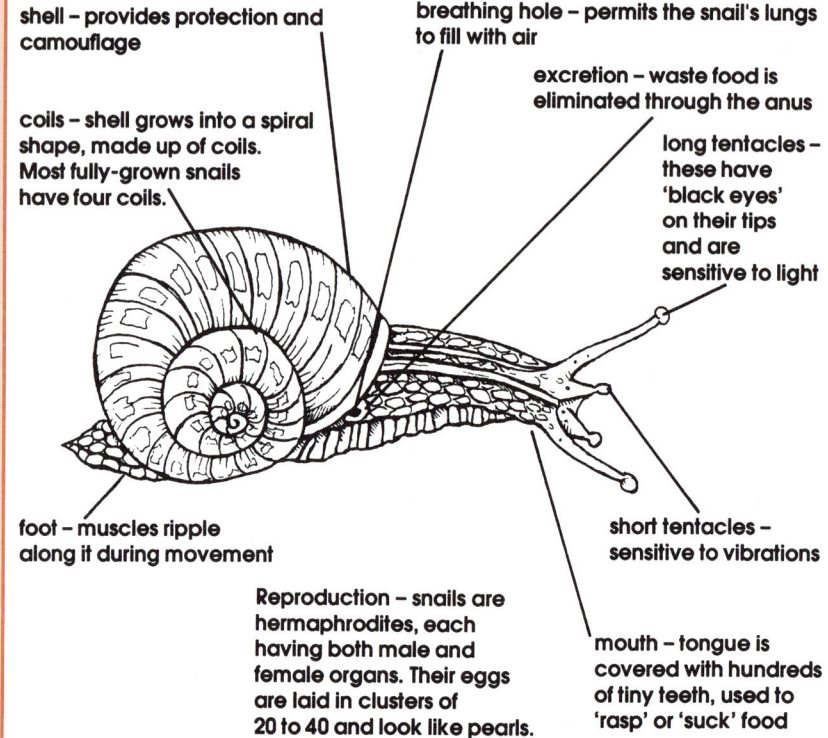

- shell – provides protection and camouflage
- coils – shell grows into a spiral shape, made up of coils. Most fully-grown snails have four coils.
- foot – muscles ripple along it during movement
- breathing hole – permits the snail's lungs to fill with air
- excretion – waste food is eliminated through the anus
- long tentacles – these have 'black eyes' on their tips and are sensitive to light
- short tentacles – sensitive to vibrations
- mouth – tongue is covered with hundreds of tiny teeth, used to 'rasp' or 'suck' food

Reproduction – snails are hermaphrodites, each having both male and female organs. Their eggs are laid in clusters of 20 to 40 and look like pearls.

Collecting and caring for snails

- Look for snails in damp places such as the undersides of leaves, in between the bricks of walls and under stones.

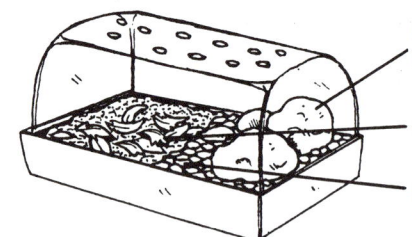

propagator

- large stones (limestone) arranged so that snails can crawl underneath
- damp soil and leaf litter (leaves on top)
- 5–8cm of gravel (keep this moist)

- Spray water on to the soil each day. Add a piece of cuttlefish bone to keep their shells strong. You can make your own snail food with this recipe:

> 1 tbs breakfast oats
> 2 tbs dried milk
> 1 tbs powdered chalk (calcium carbonate from the chemist – not blackboard chalk)
> Mix together with water to form a paste.

- Feed the snails with the paste once a day. Remove unwanted food and clean their homes once a week. You can keep your snails for several months.

What am I like?

- In the space below draw a picture of your snail. Label it carefully.

You will need:
- snail
- hand lens
- small Perspex sheet
- snail food

- Now answer the following questions on the back of this sheet:
  How does it –

  - move without legs?
  - breathe without nostrils?
  - eat?
  - get rid of waste food?
  - grow bigger?

  - hear things?
  - see things?
  - make more snails?
  - spend the winter?

- Think of some questions of your own. Make a list of them. Find out more about snails from information books.

 Wash your hands.

Snails 2 – Ideas page

Aims

- To develop the scientific skills of:
  - question-raising
  - planning and carrying out a fair test
  - controlling and measuring variables.
- To develop an understanding of movement in animals.

Background

Snails move by waves of contraction (ripples) of the muscular foot. These lift the snail slightly off the ground and push it forward. Movement is assisted by the production of a layer of thick slime all over its body but mainly at the front of its foot. This is both slippery and sticky, allowing the snail to slide along or climb on almost any surface.

Collecting and caring for your snail

- See page 10 for details. Also, spray snails with tepid water to prevent them from becoming too dry during activities. A snail that has sealed the opening to its shell has become too hot or dry and should be returned to its original environment.

Activities

- The activity page is a planning board that the children can use in groups. It includes the various stages of an investigation, including the identification and the subsequent control of variables to ensure a fair test. The children should make predictions before carrying out their investigation and try to explain any trends in their results.
- Below is an example of an investigation that could involve the use of the activity sheet. A few snails are needed for this experiment.

Investigation: does the length of a snail's foot make any difference to the speed at which it moves?

1. Measure and record the length of each snail's foot.

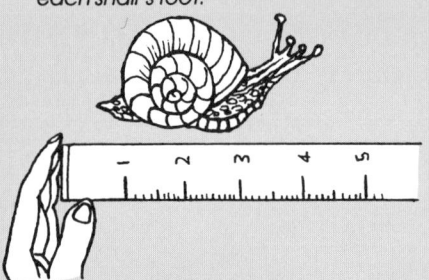

2. Spray them with tepid water to make them more active

3. Place each snail on to a piece of black sugar paper and leave it for ten minutes.

4. After ten minutes, measure the trail of slime with a piece of string.

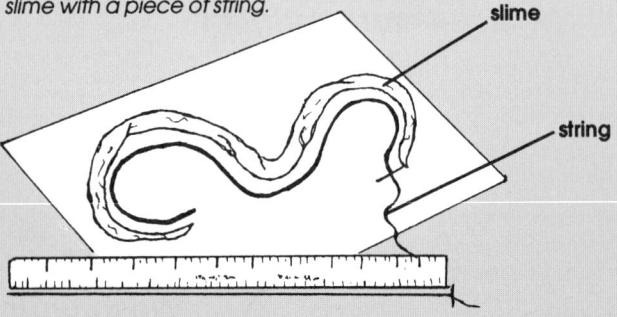

Did the snail that travelled the furthest in ten minutes have the longest foot?

Development

- Investigate the movement of snails on different surfaces. Do they show a preference?
- What do the children notice about the amount of slime produced? (The rougher the surface the more slime is produced.)

A snail investigation

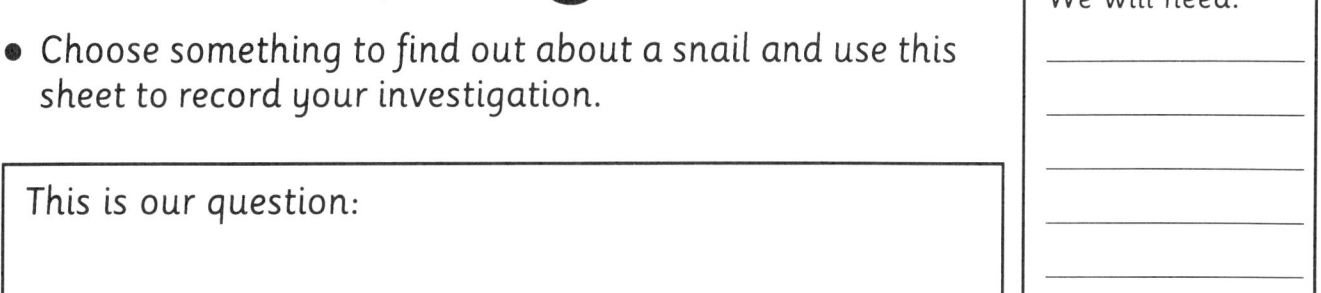

- Choose something to find out about a snail and use this sheet to record your investigation.

We will need:
_____
_____
_____
_____
_____

This is our question:

This is what we will do:

We will change:

We will measure and record:

We will not change:

This is what we predict will happen:

- Make a table and a graph to record your findings.
- What have you found out?
- Think of ways to improve your test.

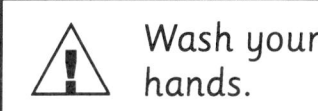

Wash your hands.

Slugs – Ideas page

Aims

- To develop concepts relating to sensitivity, habitat and movement in animals.
- To develop the skills of observing, recording, predicting, planning and investigating.

Collecting and caring for slugs

- Slugs can be found easily in the spring, summer and autumn. The best time to collect them is on rainy days. Look in long wet grass, under stones and wood and rotting leaves. They can be picked up with a piece of thin card and transferred to a small plastic container. The children must wash their hands after handling them.
- A classroom home can be made from a plastic container covered with cling film (put several air holes in the film). The container needs to have a layer of earth and some stones and pieces of wood for the slugs to crawl under. The earth should be kept damp but not soggy. The container should be kept cool, away from radiators and out of the sun. Slugs can be fed carrot or apple. Any slug that is especially slow-moving may have become dehydrated. It will need to be sprinkled with water and left in its home to recover. Slugs should be returned to their natural environment after about one week.

Background

Slugs have a soft body, no legs, two pairs of tentacles and a mantle. They are molluscs belonging to the class called Gastropoda ('belly-footed') and the subclass Pulmonata ('having lungs'). Slugs are hermaphrodites, having both male and female sex organs. Although initially disliked by many children, they do provide a fascinating opportunity to study invertebrate life.

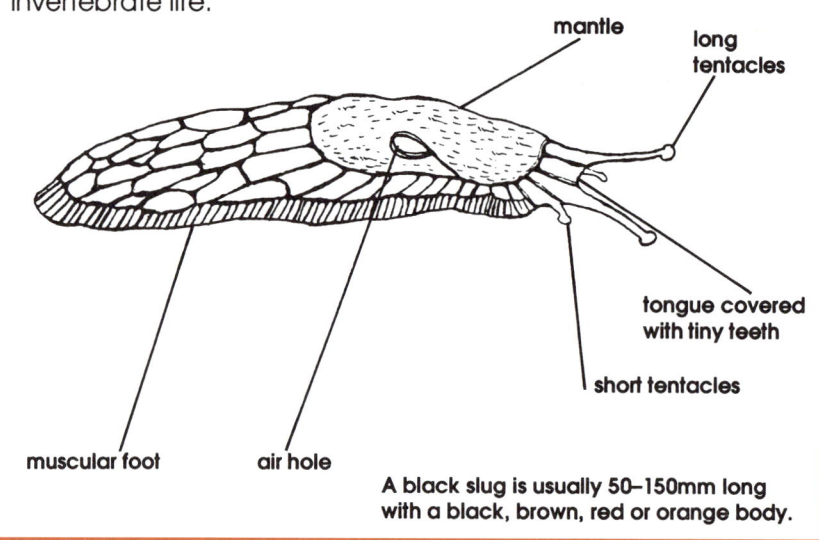

A black slug is usually 50–150mm long with a black, brown, red or orange body.

Activities

- The activity will enable the children to investigate whether or not slugs can smell. Suitable materials for testing are coffee, vinegar, mint, orange squash and washing-up liquid.
- Make a large version of the activity sheet and place the materials on the circumference.
- Place the slug on the centre of the circle and record on the activity sheet which material it moves towards.
- Do this test a few times with the same slug, then try others.
  - Do they all move to the same material?
  - Which material do they seem to prefer?
  - Which do they never go to?

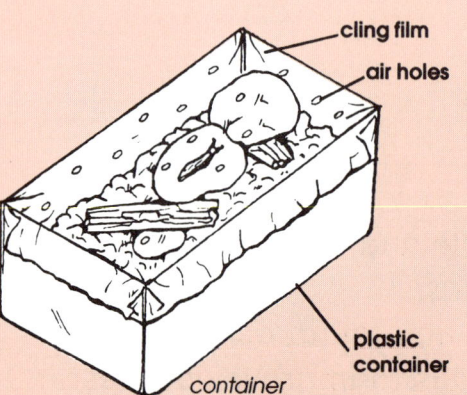

Development

- Further investigations can be carried out to see:
  - how they react to light shining on them
  - how they react to touch (use a soft brush)
  - how they react to different sounds.

Can slugs smell?

- Place your slug in the centre of the circle.
- Record your observations.

You will need:
- slugs
- coffee
- vinegar
- mint
- orange squash
- washing-up liquid

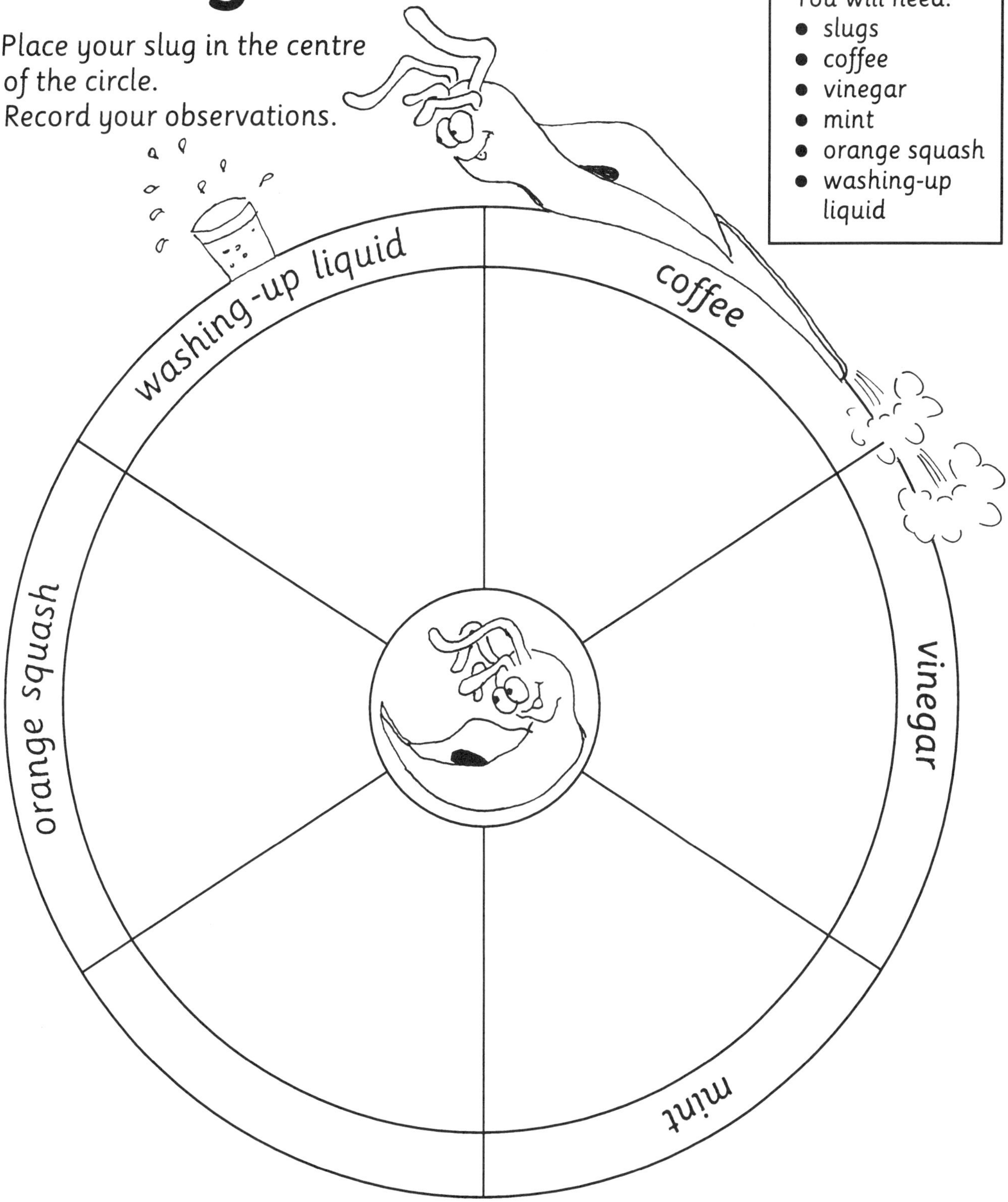

(circle labelled with: washing-up liquid, coffee, vinegar, mint, orange squash)

- Why do you think the slug reacted the way it did?
- Are there any ways to improve the test?
- How could you find out if slugs are sensitive to light, touch or sound?

Wash your hands.

Earthworms – Ideas page

Aims

- To develop understanding of movement and other life processes of animals.
- To develop the skills of observing, planning, investigating and recording.

Background

Earthworms belong to a group of animals called annelids. Their bodies are cylindrical and segmented. They move using muscular contractions and extensions with the help of bristle-like chaetae. They respond to a strong light, vibrations and touch. Earthworms eat their way through the earth, extracting nutrients and expelling fine soil. Their burrowing helps to aerate and drain the soil.

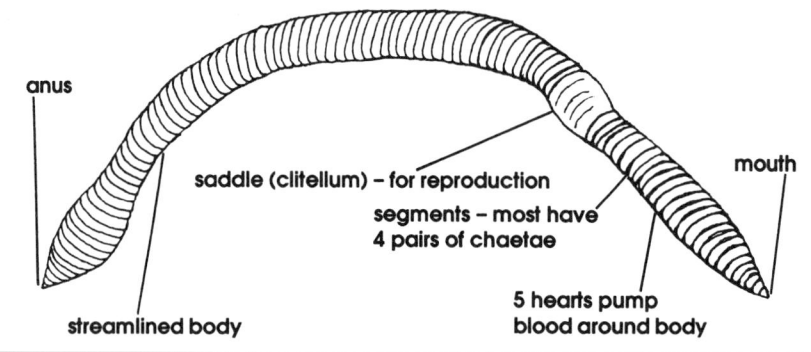

Collecting and caring for earthworms

- Earthworms can be found in loose, dampish earth. Encourage them to come to the surface by pouring soapy water (washing-up liquid) over the earth, or by stamping on the ground for several minutes. They should be rinsed in clean water.
- If possible, provide a wormery to observe them tunnelling and mixing up the soil. This should contain layers of different-coloured soils with leaves on the surface. Cover the wormery with black polythene for a few days. When removed the tunnels made in the soil should be clearly seen.
- Alternatively, make a classroom home for the worms by placing the bottom section of a plastic bottle inside a clear plastic jar and putting layers of different-coloured soils around the bottle, so that the worms do not move to the middle of the jar and can be observed. The entire home should be covered with black paper.

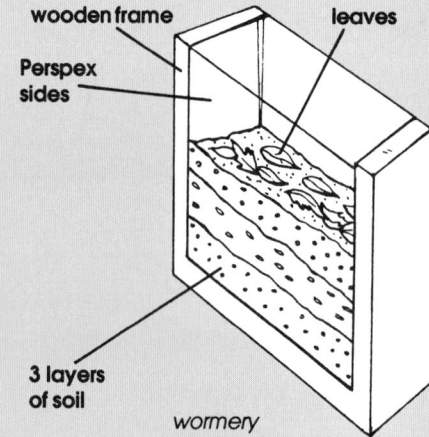

wormery

Development

- Investigate how the earthworms move on different surfaces.
- Other investigations could be:
  - Can earthworms smell?
  - Do earthworms respond to sound?
  - What do earthworms prefer to eat?
  - Do they prefer damp or dry soil?
  - Are they sensitive to light?
  - Where would you find the most worms?

Activities

- To observe and record how earthworms move, carry out the following:
  - The worms should be placed on damp blotting paper.
  - References should be made to body segments, saddle, skin and bristles. There are several different types of earthworm and the children should be encouraged to observe and record any differences between those they have collected.

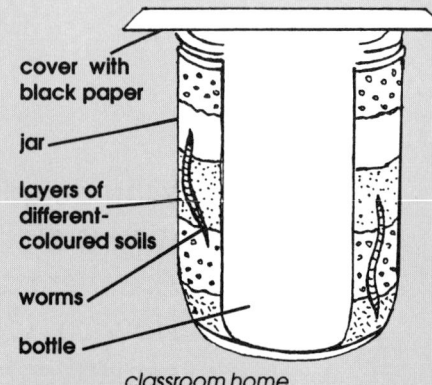

classroom home

IDEAS BANK – Minibeasts

How do earthworms move?

 Don't let your worms get too dry.
Don't leave them in the light for too long.
After about 20 minutes put your worms back into damp earth.

You will need:
- earthworms
- damp blotting paper
- pencil
- ruler
- Perspex
- wood
- polythene
- piece of carpet
- corrugated cardboard
- newspaper

- Place an earthworm on some damp blotting paper. Watch carefully to see what happens as it moves. Give your worm a name and draw a comic strip to show how it moves. Write a sentence under each drawing to describe what is happening.

- Measure the length of your earthworm at its longest _____ cm.

- Measure the length of your earthworm at its shortest _____ cm.

- The difference in length = _____ cm.

 • Find out what kind of surface earthworms move best on. Try materials such as Perspex, wood, polythene, paper, carpet, corrugated cardboard and newspaper. Can you hear the bristles scratching as your worm moves?

 Wash your hands.

Woodlice – Ideas page

Aim

- To develop:
  - understanding of movement and nutrition in animals
  - the concepts of habitat and how animals adapt to their environment
  - understanding of animal behaviour
  - the scientific skills of predicting, observing, planning, investigating, recording and drawing conclusions.

Background

Woodlice belong to the group of animals called arthropods. Behavioural scientists have discovered that woodlice move away from unsuitable environments by making a series of right and left turns. A left turn is usually followed by a right turn. The children might find this pattern is apparent in their maze tests.

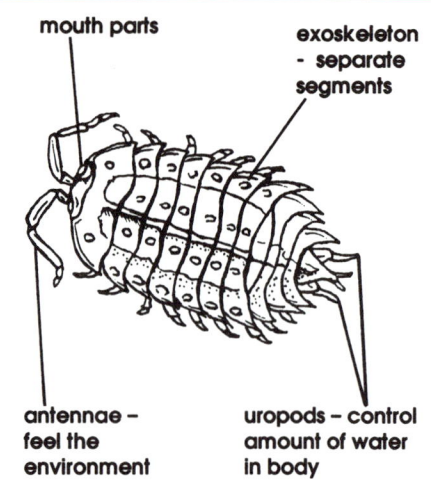

Activities

- The children should observe the woodlice as they move around a shallow container and look for similarities and differences. Point out the legs and antennae.
- They should construct mazes, first simple and then more complex. They could use cardboard, building blocks or interlocking cubes to do this. They should look for patterns in the movement of the woodlice through the mazes.

Collecting and caring for woodlice

- Woodlice can be found in a variety of places - under dead tree bark, stones and bricks, rotting damp leaves and around the bottom of trees. When collecting them the children should use a plastic spoon or a piece of paper to gently lift the woodlice into a container with a lid. A classroom home can be made from a container lined with plaster of Paris.

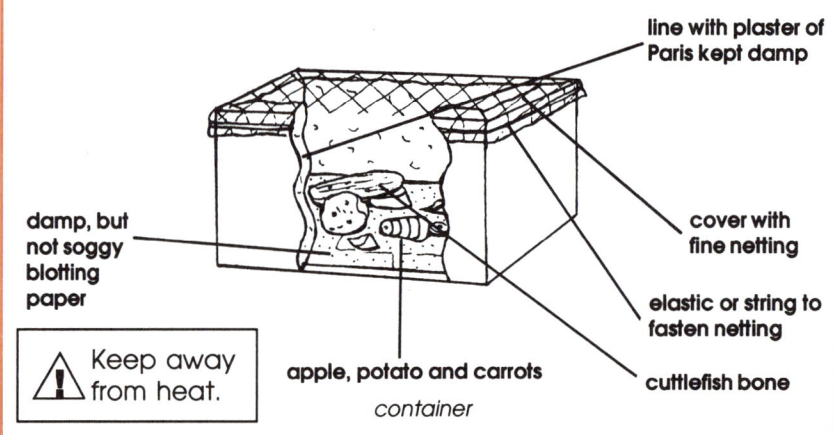

container

Development

- Other investigations might be:
  - finding food preferences. The children should devise an investigation where the woodlice (nocturnal feeders) are offered a choice of foods
  - finding out what conditions woodlice prefer (such as damp, dry, dark or light), using a choice chamber.

They should make predictions first. Don't keep woodlice where they are not happy.
- Place ten woodlice in the choice chamber and cover the whole chamber. After one hour look to see where the woodlice are.
- Ask the children to find out where woodlice live in their natural environment.

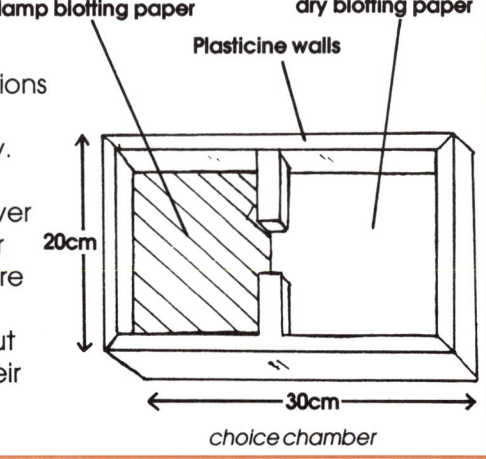

choice chamber

On the move

- In the space below, draw and label a woodlouse.

You will need:
- woodlice
- cardboard
- plastic building blocks
- Plasticine
- 1cm square wood

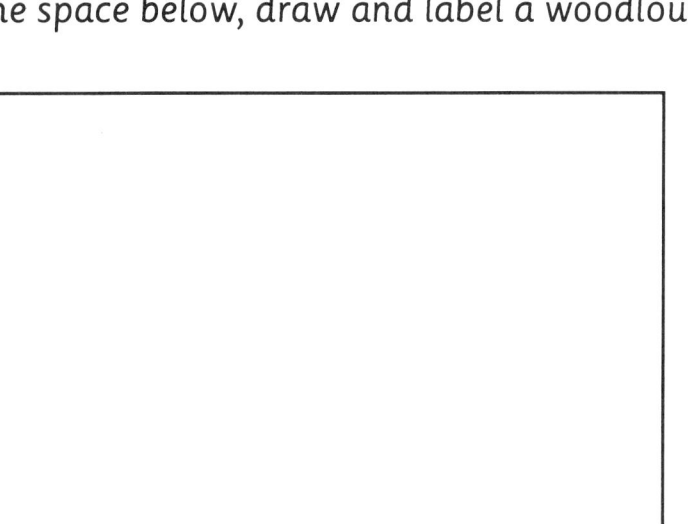

⚠ Remember … always return the woodlice to their home in your classroom after about 30 minutes. Remember to wash your hands.

- Watch some woodlice move around. How do they use their legs and their antennae?

- Make a simple maze like this one and put some woodlice in it.

- Record their movements on this maze.

- Can you see any pattern?

- Do they all move in the same direction?

- Describe how your woodlouse moves through the maze.

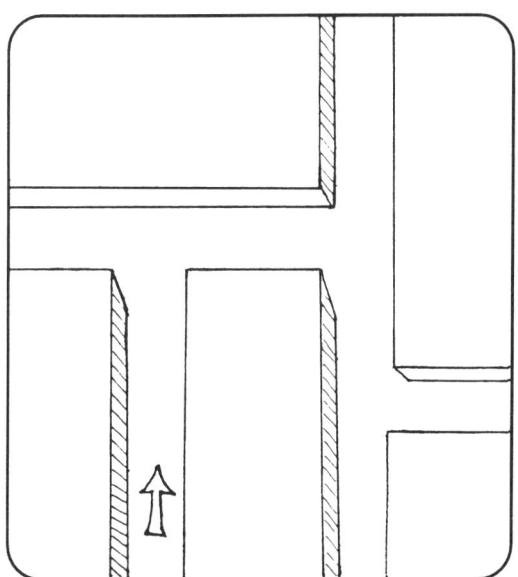

Use a different-coloured pencil for each woodlouse's journey.

- Build a maze with more turns. Do you notice anything different about the way the woodlice move? What conclusions can you make?

© Folens (copiable page)   IDEAS BANK – *Minibeasts*

Stick insects – Ideas page

Aims

- To understand that some animals have an exoskeleton as opposed to an endoskeleton.
- To understand incomplete metamorphosis.

Activities

- The children should observe the stick insect and produce a detailed drawing.
- They should then label the parts of the human body.
- They should detect similarities and differences between the stick insect and themselves by observing characteristics and the two skeletal systems.
- Using information books, encourage the children to record the process of ecdysis and discuss the stick insect's life cycle.

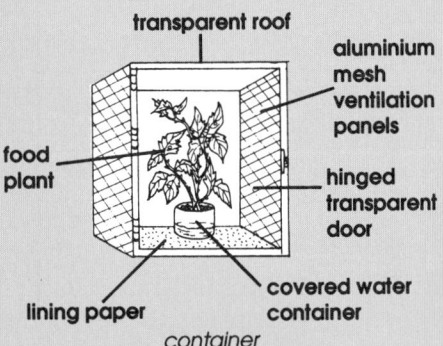
container

Development

- Investigate the walking behaviour of stick insects.
- Test food preferences.
- Construct a growth chart (revealing the dramatic growth spurt following each skin change).

Background

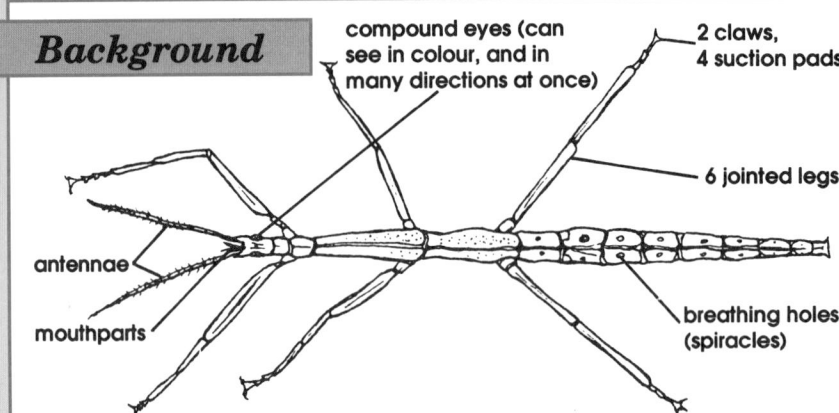

Stick insects belong to the order Phasmida. They have a head, thorax and abdomen and can be winged or wingless. They have a cuticle (exoskeleton) and live for approximately one year. Some species reproduce sexually (mating occurs between male and female) while others reproduce by parthenogenesis (without fertilisation by a male). They exhibit both passive (being camouflaged to resemble a twig) and active (red warning colouration, release of fluid, stabbing and hissing) defence mechanisms. Their life cycle is an example of incomplete metamorphosis whereby the nymph resembles the adult throughout the stages of growth – the adult form develops gradually without any sudden change in body shape.

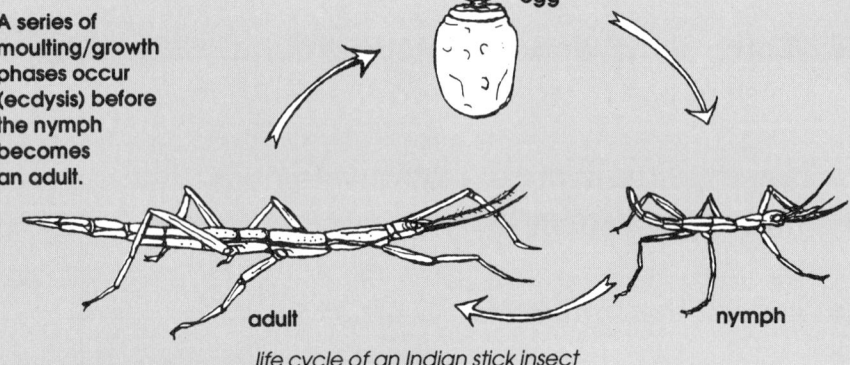
life cycle of an Indian stick insect

Collecting and caring for stick insects

- The Indian and Pink-winged stick insects are the best to keep and are available from pet shops. They are not native to Britain. To allow ecdysis (the shedding of skin to allow growth) to occur successfully, the stick insects (approximately 20) need to be housed in a tall (at least 45cm), well-ventilated cage in a warm room. Avoid windowsills where there can be extreme temperatures. The Indian variety can be fed on privet, bramble or ivy leaves and the Pink-winged will eat bramble. The sprigs should be changed every three days and the new ones sprayed with a fine mist of water each day. The lining of the base of any container should be changed once a week and all corpses, leaves, skins and unwanted eggs discarded.

What's the difference?

- Draw and label your stick insect. Use a hand lens to help you.

You will need:
- stick insect
- ruler
- tape measure
- hand lens

My stick insect is _____ cm long. It has a skeleton on the _____ of its body. This is called a c _____ .

Label the parts of the skeleton below.

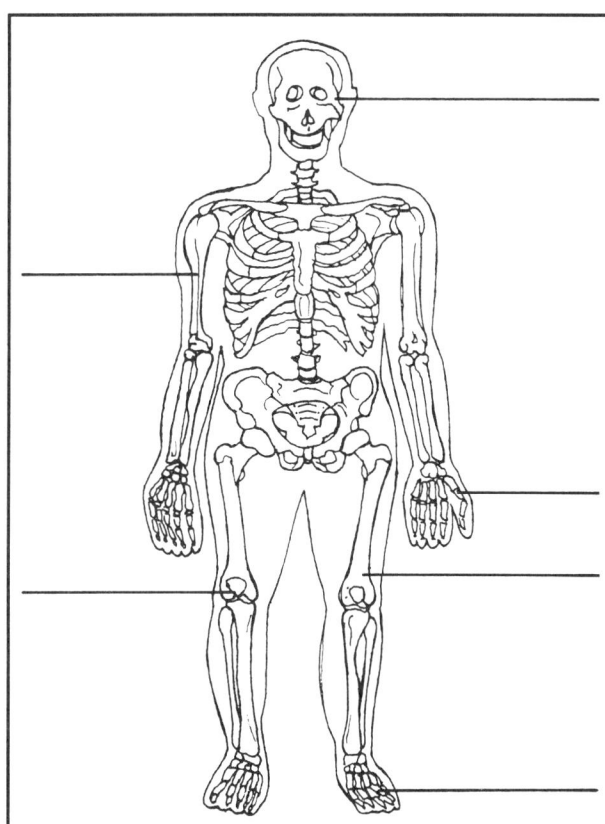

- Look at the two pictures. Which things are:

... the same?

... different?

My height is _____ cm. I have a skeleton on the _____ of my body. As I grow my skeleton _____ .

 • Find out what happens to a stick insect's skeleton as the stick insect grows.

 Wash your hands.

© Folens (copiable page)   IDEAS BANK – *Minibeasts*   21

Caterpillars – Ideas page

Aims

- To develop understanding of nutrition, growth and movement in animals.
- To develop the scientific skills of observing, recording and carrying out investigations.
- To develop technological skills relating to designing and making a device.

Background

There are many different kinds of caterpillars. They are insects belonging to the group of animals called arthropods. All caterpillars have soft bodies with 13 segments. They have six true legs at the front of their bodies and up to ten false legs (prolegs).

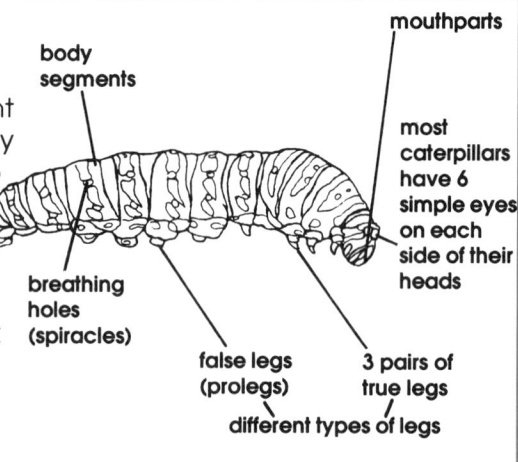

Collecting and caring for caterpillars

- Caterpillars can be found, in late spring and summer, on plants such as stinging nettles, cabbages, docks, holly, ivy and hawthorn trees. Some can cause skin-irritation so it is best not to touch them. Use a soft, damp paintbrush or a piece of paper to move them. Only collect a few at a time, with the right food plant for them. Place the caterpillar and food plant in a plastic box before transferring it to a classroom home.
- A classroom home for caterpillars needs to be large and airy. They are voracious eaters and should be kept supplied with fresh leaves. Clean the container weekly and keep it at room temperature away from the sun. Return the caterpillars to where you found them when you have finished with them.

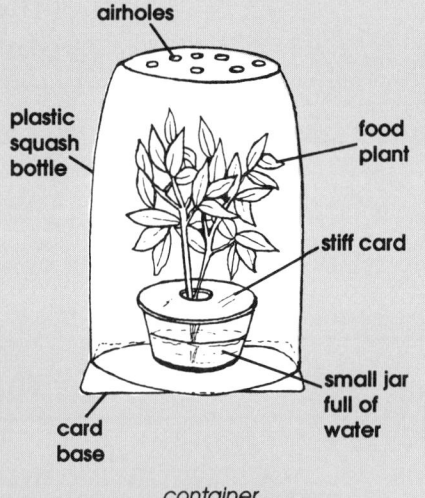

container

Activities

- Find out how much and when caterpillars eat. This can be done in pairs or small groups. One child should be the recorder.
- After three days discuss any findings.
  - Were the tests fair?
  - Did the children leave the caterpillar on its leaf for the same amount of time each day?

Development

- Let the children use a magnifier to observe a caterpillar and complete a chart such as the one on the right.
- Use a damp brush to place the caterpillar on a piece of paper and watch how it moves. How far does it move in two minutes?
- Measure the length of a caterpillar daily. Plot a graph to show changes. Is there a pattern?
- Design and construct a sensitive device to weigh a caterpillar. Use it to measure any daily changes in its weight.

My caterpillar	
How many segments (sections) does its body have?	
What colour is it?	
Is it hairy?	
How long is it?	
Are there air holes (spiracles) along the body?	
How many legs does it have?	
Are there any mouthparts?	
Are there any eyes?	

Caterpillars and food

You will need:
- caterpillars
- food leaves
- cm square paper
- pencil
- transparent container

Draw around a food leaf on centimetre square paper.

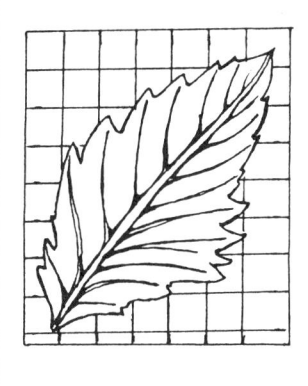

Put the food leaf into a small transparent container with one caterpillar.

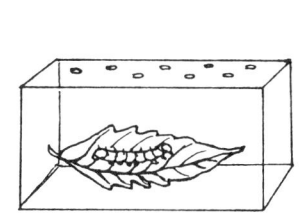

After a few hours put the leaf back on the paper and draw around what is left of the leaf.

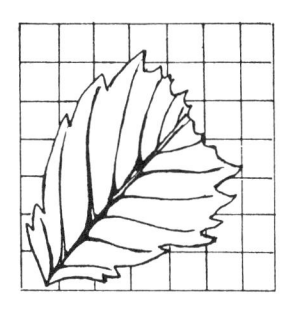

How many square centimetres of leaf has the caterpillar eaten?

_____ cm²

- Investigate how much caterpillars eat at different times of the day.
- Record your findings.

	Day 1		Day 2		Day 3	
	morning	afternoon	morning	afternoon	morning	afternoon
caterpillar 1						
caterpillar 2						
caterpillar 3						
caterpillar 4						

- What did you find out?
- Is your test fair? Does the number of caterpillars you test make any difference?
- How could you find out if they eat more in the dark than in the light?

 Wash your hands.

Butterflies – Ideas page

Aims

- To develop understanding of movement and sensitivity in animals.
- To develop the scientific skills of observation and drawing conclusions.

Activities

- Discuss the different flowers that the children have seen butterflies on or near.
  - What colours are the flowers?
  - Do they think butterflies visit every flower?
  - What do they think attracts the butterfly to or makes it stay away from a specific flower?
- Organise the children into groups and give each group a copy of the activity sheet. Read the sheet through with them and ask them to carry out the investigation and record their findings.

Development

- Go on to do a similar test for scent.
- Observation of butterflies could include the following:
  - What colour are the wings?
  - What is the body like?
  - What flowers do they feed on?
  - How do the wings move when they are flying?
  - When are they most active?

Background

Butterflies are insects belonging to the group of animals called arthropods. There are many different kinds of butterflies but all of their bodies have three parts – a head, a thorax and an abdomen. They each have two pairs of wings, six legs and two antennae. They start life as an egg and then change into a caterpillar, then to a pupa and finally change to an adult. This process is called complete metamorphosis (change in shape). Some butterflies can fly great distances. Some species spend the winter in Africa and migrate north in the spring in order to find suitable plants for their caterpillars to feed on.

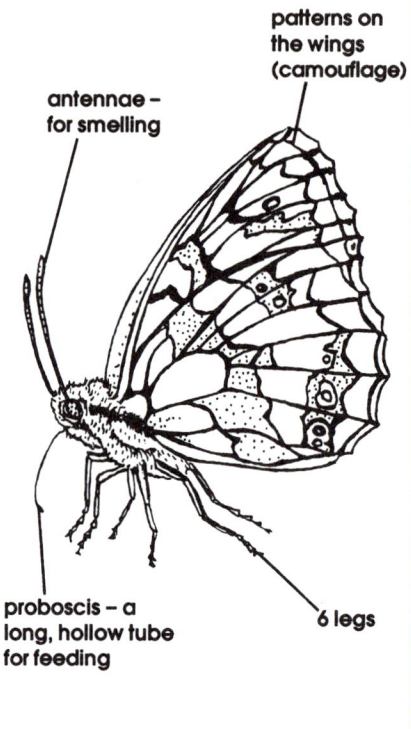

egg   caterpillar   pupa   adult

Collecting and caring for butterflies

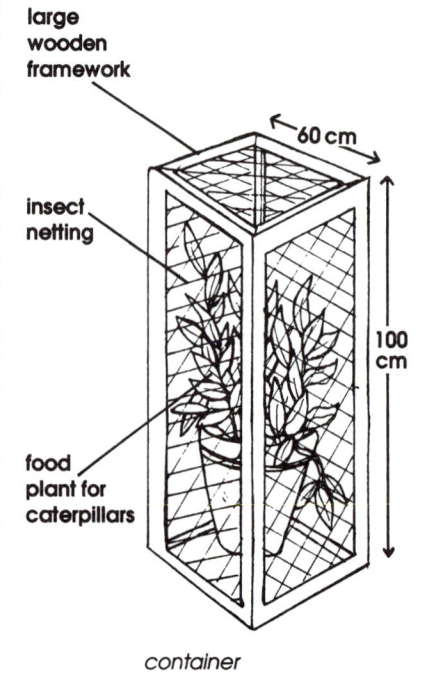

- Some species of butterflies have become quite scarce so it is best not to try to collect them. They can be observed in the wild during the summer months or they can be reared from eggs in the classroom. A local secondary school biology teacher will be able to give you the address of an egg supplier. You will need to construct a breeding cage. This will enable the children to witness the dramatic life-cycle changes as the caterpillars change to adults. Feed butterflies by giving them fresh flowers, such as lilac, or some cotton-wool buds soaked in a honey and water solution. (1 spoonful of honey to 10 spoonfuls of water).

Butterflies and colour

- Make five different-coloured paper flowers.
- Place the flowers in your breeding cage or where there are a lot of butterflies.
- First, predict which flower you think will be visited the most times.
- Observe the flowers for 30 minutes.
- Record the number of times a butterfly lands or goes near a flower.

You will need:
- butterflies
- tissue paper
- honey
- sugar
- vinegar
- cheese

colour of flower	red	blue	yellow	pink	orange
visits to the flower					
totals					

- What do your results suggest?

_____

_____

- Plan a test to see if butterflies are attracted by scent. Use materials such as honey, sugar, vinegar and cheese. Make your test fair. Repeat your test. What do your results suggest?

 Wash your hands.

Ants – Ideas page

Aims

- To develop concepts relating to the life processes of movement, nutrition and sensitivity.
- To develop concepts relating to habitats and interdependence.
- To develop the scientific skills of observation, recording and investigating.

Background

There are thousands of different types of ants throughout the world and over 40 different kinds in Britain. They are arthropods and belong to the class known as Insecta. As social insects they are closely related to bees and wasps.

They have a hard exoskeleton, three body parts, two antennae, six jointed legs and a thin waist between their abdomen and thorax. Most ants do not have wings but queens and males have two pairs. They use their wings during mating. Ants live in nests or colonies, with different ants having different jobs to do. Some ants squirt a weak acid to defend themselves, so when handling them ensure that hands are thoroughly washed afterwards.

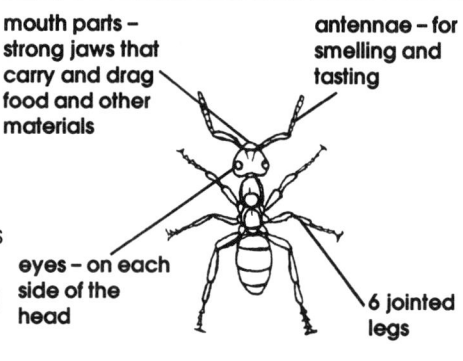

Activities

- Observe the behaviour of the ants in a formicarium.
- Divide the class into groups and allocate a specific time each day to each group. They should watch the ants for around 15 minutes.
- Ask one child from each group to record the findings on the activity sheet.

Collecting and caring for ants

- During the spring and summer ants can be found under paving slabs and other large stones, as well as in the earth and near plants such as roses and thistles. The children should wear gloves when collecting them, using small plastic containers and damp paintbrushes. To keep ants for longer than two days an ant home called a formicarium (from the Latin word 'formica' which means ant) needs to be built. A colony, including a queen, will need to be collected. To observe them with a magnifier it is worth slowing down their movements by placing them in a refrigerator for a few minutes. This is like a cold night for them and is not harmful.

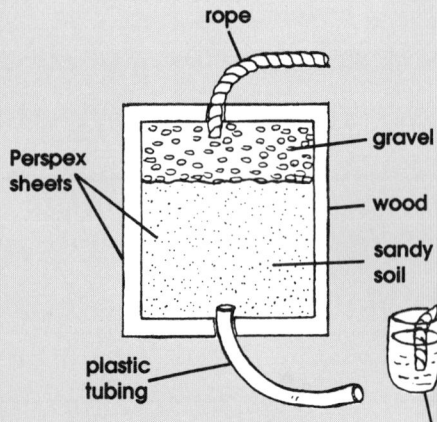

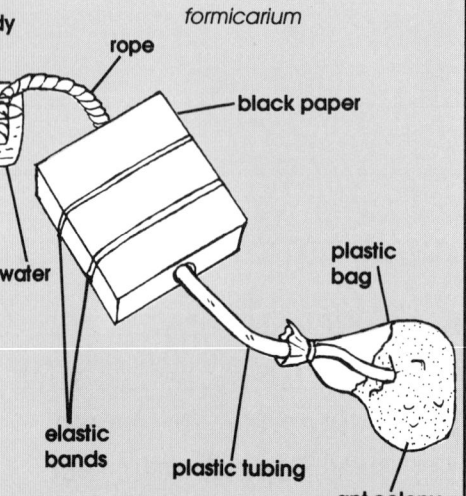

formicarium

To make a formicarium

- Place a wooden frame on to a sheet of Perspex. Put sand and gravel inside the frame and place a second Perspex sheet on top. Secure at the corners. Drill holes in the frame for a piece of rope and some tubing.
- Put the end of the rope into water and the end of the tubing into a plastic bag containing the ants.
- Cover the frame with black paper and shine a torch on to the plastic bag. The ants will move into the formicarium.
- Fill the bag with food such as sugar.

Development

- Investigate food preferences. Try bread, cheese, fruit, sugar and cereals.
- Ask the children to devise a test to see whether ants can hear.

Ant behaviour

Observe ants in a formicarium.
- How do they carry things?
- What do they do when they meet each other?
- Do they ever fight?
- Record your observations every day for a week.

You will need:
- ants
- formicarium

 Wash your hands.

Monday	
Tuesday	
Wednesday	
Thursday	
Friday	

- Investigate which type of food they prefer to eat.

to formicarium — plastic tube — place different foods in plastic bag

© Folens (copiable page)   IDEAS BANK – Minibeasts

Earwigs – Ideas page

Aims

- To develop concepts relating to habitat and movement.
- To develop the scientific skills of observation, investigation, planning and recording.

Activities

- The activity sheet asks whether earwigs prefer small places. In fact, they do prefer places where their bodies are in contact with something solid. This preference is called thigmokinesis.
- Prepare a solid piece of wood by drilling it with progressively larger holes. Do not drill right through the block. The bottom of each hole should be at the same height from the base of the block of wood. Place the block in a deep tray to prevent escape.
- Put at least ten earwigs near to the block of wood and observe them.
- Repeat this each day for a week. Ask the children to record their findings and draw conclusions. Discuss why it would be 'unfair' if the holes were at varying heights and why the test is repeated.

Development

- Carry out experiments to see, for example, whether earwigs prefer light or dark, damp or dry places.
- Make a detailed labelled drawing of an earwig.

Background

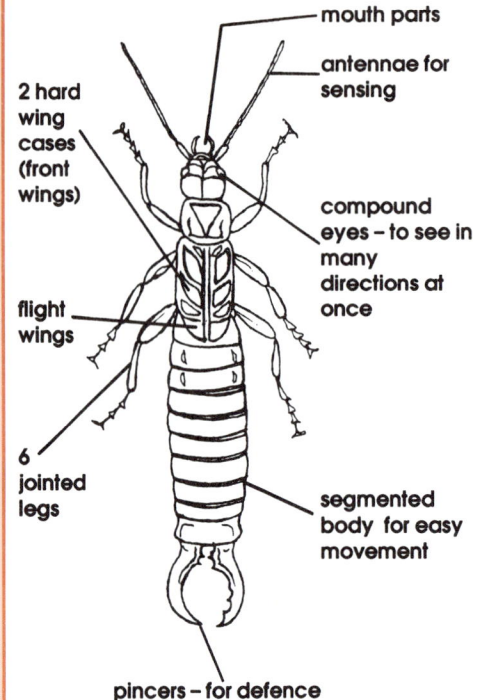

Earwigs are beautiful insects with three body parts (head, thorax and abdomen), three pairs of jointed legs, two antennae, two pairs of wings (wing cases and flight wings) and a pair of pincers at the back end. The flight wings are very large and are folded to fit under the wing cases.

Earwigs don't fly often, but when they do they have a difficult task to fold their flight wings back under their wing cases.

Their mouthparts have biting jaws with sharp cutting edges. These jaws are also used by the earwig to clean itself.

Collecting and caring for earwigs

- The children should have small containers and soft, damp paint brushes for collecting earwigs. This should be carried out in the late summer and autumn when earwigs are most abundant. They can be found in old buildings, inside flowers such as marigolds and under bark. They can be attracted by providing places for them to shelter in, such as upturned flowerpots. In some areas, the children will find many earwigs but in others it may be difficult to find even one.
- A plastic container, such as an ice-cream tub, will make a suitable home. They need to be fed a variety of foods, such as fruit and potatoes. Do not let the food go mouldy. Keep the container at room temperature away from direct heat. Release them into their own environment after ten days.

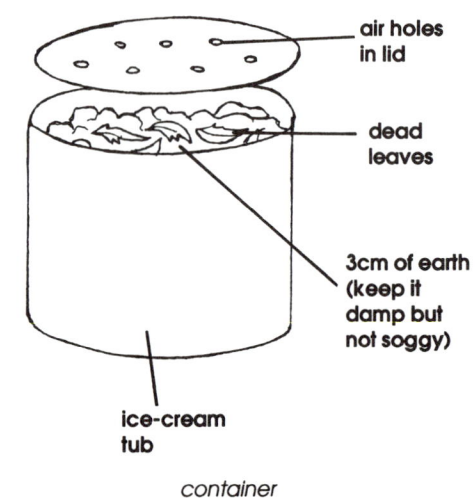

container

Earwigs

- Do earwigs prefer small or large places?
- Predict first, then carry out this experiment.
- Make a wooden block with a series of different sized holes drilled into it. These must be the same height from the base.

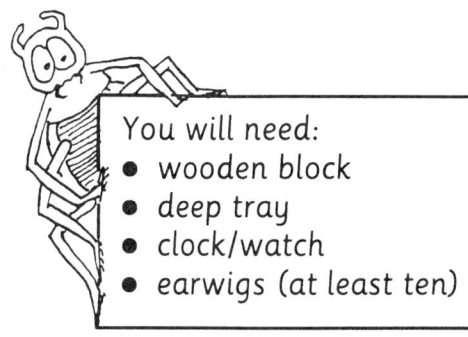

You will need:
- wooden block
- deep tray
- clock/watch
- earwigs (at least ten)

What do you think will happen?

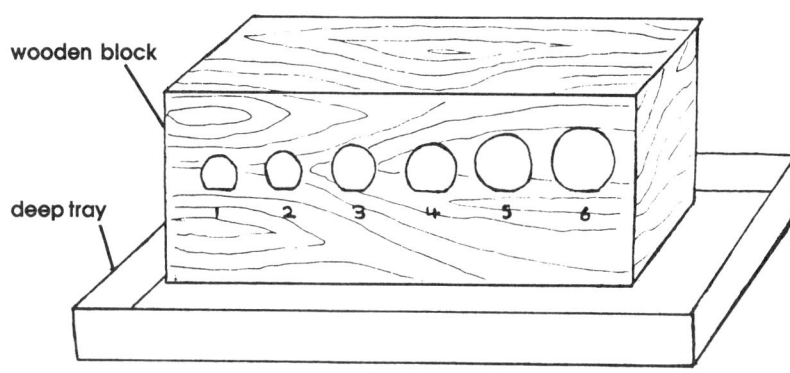

hole test

Hole	Monday	Tuesday	Wednesday	Thursday	Friday
1					
2					
3					
4					
5					
6					
Still in tray					

- What did you discover?
- How did you make your test fair?
- Why use more than one earwig?

- Find out if earwigs prefer high or low places. Remember to make your test fair.

Wash your hands.

© Folens (copiable page)　　　IDEAS BANK – *Minibeasts*　　　29

Aphids – Ideas page

Aims

- To develop scientific concepts relating to diversity of species, distribution and habitat.
- To develop scientific skills of observation, investigating, recording and drawing conclusions.

Activities

- The activity sheet enables children to record their investigations into whether aphids prefer sunny places to shady places. This activity would be an ideal homework study.
- If this sheet is to be used at home, suggest alternatives for those children without gardens. For example, these children might work in a suitable area in the school grounds. Alternatively, they could perform this activity with a friend who has a garden.
- When the children have a copy of the sheet, discuss with them exactly what they have to do.
- Discuss why they need to make sure the test is fair.

Development

- Take this activity a stage further and identify the parts of a plant that aphids prefer.
- Look for winged and wingless aphids and their favoured habitats.
- Do aphids move around much while they are on plants?

Background

Aphids are frequently referred to as 'greenfly' or 'blackfly'. They are not flies but a common kind of bug. As insects they belong to an order called Hemiptera (meaning 'half-winged'). They have very small bodies, six jointed legs, long antennae, mouth parts which are tube-like and a pair of cornicles near their back ends. The cornicles are used for protection, squirting offensive liquids when attacked. Aphids are the only insects with cornicles. The mouth tube is called a proboscis and it is used to suck sap from plants. There are hundreds of different kinds of aphids and some have two pairs of wings. The life-cycles of aphids are unusual in two ways. Firstly, and unusually among minibeasts, they give birth to live young. This is called viviparity. Secondly, female aphids can give birth without mating. This is called parthenogenesis.

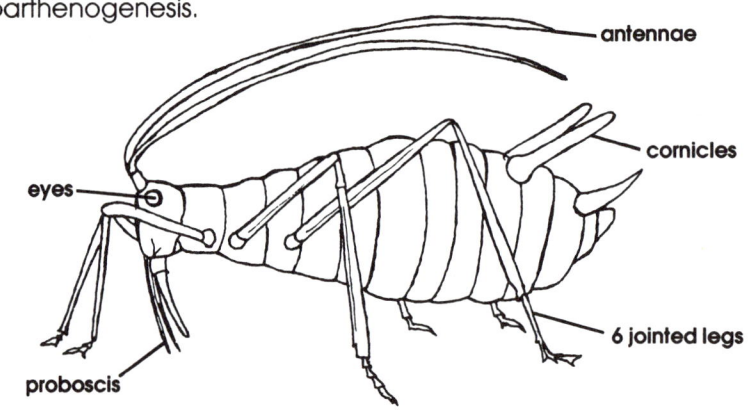

Collecting and caring for aphids

Aphids can be found during the spring and summer on plants such as roses and nasturtiums. In a vegetable garden children should look on cabbages, runner beans and broad beans. They can be observed, using a suitable magnifier, while they are feeding on plants. They need to be collected with their food plant. The food plant should be placed in water within a transparent container. As aphids are plant-damaging pests care should be taken so that they don't escape.

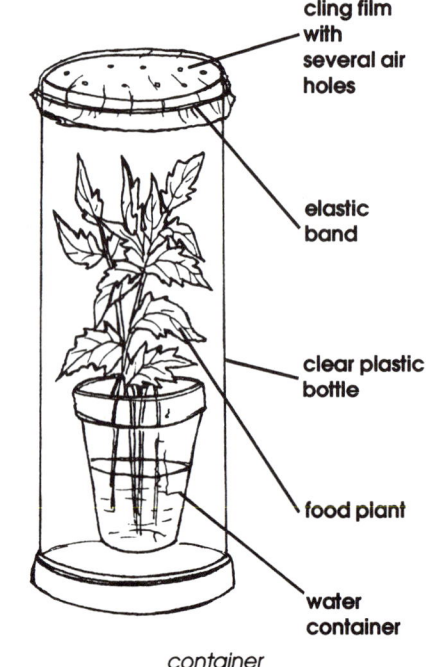

container

Do aphids prefer sun or shade?

You will need:
- access to garden with roses and nasturtiums
- clipboard
- pencil

- First, predict which you think they prefer.
- On the back of this sheet sketch a plan of the area that you will be studying. It needs to have plants such as roses or vegetables in it.
- Note the time and then label the sunny parts and shady parts of the area. Choose ten plants and mark them on your plan.
- To make it a fair test, make sure that:
  - five plants are in a sunny place
  - five plants are in a shady place
  - all the plants are healthy
  - all the plants are similar in size
  - you count the aphids at the same time every day.
- Record your results on the chart below.

I predict that:

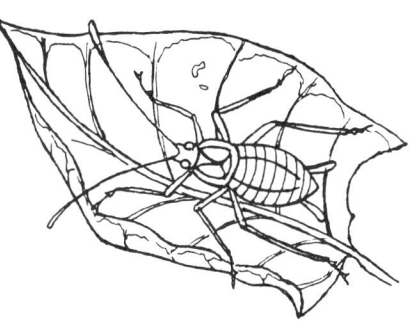

Number of aphids on the plants						
Plant number	Sun			Shade		
	Day 1	Day 2	Day 3	Day 1	Day 2	Day 3
1						
2						
3						
4						
5						

 Plan an investigation to find out which part of a plant aphids like best.

 Wash your hands.

© Folens (copiable page)   IDEAS BANK – *Minibeasts*

Beetles – Ideas page

Aims

- To develop scientific concepts relating to habitat, movement and sensitivity.
- To develop the scientific skill of planning investigations.

Activities

- The children should investigate in pairs or small groups where beetles can be found.
- They should place pitfall traps around their designated area, checking them daily over a number of days.
- They might conclude where beetles like to live, checking their findings with a reference book.

Development

- Give the beetles a choice of conditions to see which they prefer:
  – damp or dry places?
  – dark or light places?
- Investigate how well they move up slopes.
- Find out if they move faster on smooth surfaces than on rough surfaces.

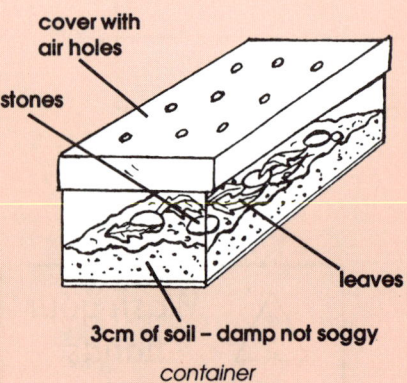
container

Background

There are more types of beetle than any other group of animals. They are found all over the world and belong to the group of animals called arthropods. All adult beetles have two antennae, six jointed legs, biting mouth parts and a hard exoskeleton to which muscles are attached. Most beetles have two pairs of wings, although some have none and do not fly. Some beetles are regarded as pests; they spread tree diseases, eat crops and gnaw wood. Other beetles are seen as helpful because they control garden pests and act as scavengers.

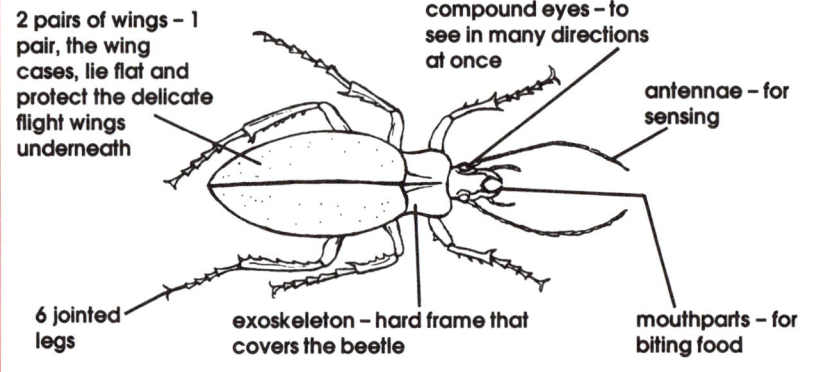

Collecting and caring for beetles

- Beetles can be found near tree stumps, compost, bark and amongst plants and grass. A good time to look for them is from April to September. Children should use a piece of thin card or a damp paintbrush to help them collect beetles. They should then be placed carefully in small plastic containers for transportation back to the classroom.

collecting

- Another collecting method is to place a small plastic pot in the ground. Use bait such as meat or fruit and carefully cover the top of the pot with a small stone. Check inside the pot daily to see what has been caught.
- For classroom investigations the beetles should be housed in a transparent plastic container, kept at room temperature away from the sun. They should not be kept for longer than two days. Pages 44–48 in this book can be used along with information books to help identify the beetles that have been collected.

32   IDEAS BANK – *Minibeasts*   © Folens

Where do beetles live?

You will need:
- small plastic containers
- damp paintbrush
- piece of card
- bait (meat or fruit)
- pencil
- stones
- plastic pot
- gardening trowel

- Select an area in your school grounds or nearby where you think beetles could be found.
- Draw a plan of the chosen area for your beetle search. Mark on the plan any trees, paths, grassy areas, bushes and other details that you can see.

- Place some pitfall traps around the area. Check them daily. When you find a beetle collect it and mark the place on your map.

pitfall trap

- Devise some experiments to find out which of the following beetles like:
    - damp places
    - dry places
    - light places
    - dark places.

Wash your hands.

© Folens (copiable page)   IDEAS BANK – *Minibeasts*

Ladybirds – Ideas page

Aims

- To develop concepts relating to reproduction, nutrition, movement, growth and life-cycle.
- To develop the scientific skills of observing and recording.

Activities

- This activity usually takes four or five weeks to complete. The sheet is suitable for use by individuals or pairs.
- The children should observe and record what happens during a ladybird's life cycle.
- A stereo microscope (binocular) allows the children to closely observe three-dimensional objects.

stereo microscope

Development

- Observe the behaviour of ladybirds, including flight.
- Investigate their preference for light or dark conditions.
- Make a frieze or model of the life-cycle of a ladybird.

Background

Ladybirds are a kind of beetle belonging to the class Insecta of the Arthropoda division. Their colourful body is nearly circular with a hard exoskeleton. The colour acts as a form of defence, especially from birds. They have two pairs of wings (flight wings at the back and hard wing cases at the front), two antennae and six jointed legs. The legs have an offensive liquid squeezed on to them when danger threatens – a good reason for the children to wash their hands after handling them. Ladybirds eat aphids and are eaten, in turn, by birds and spiders.

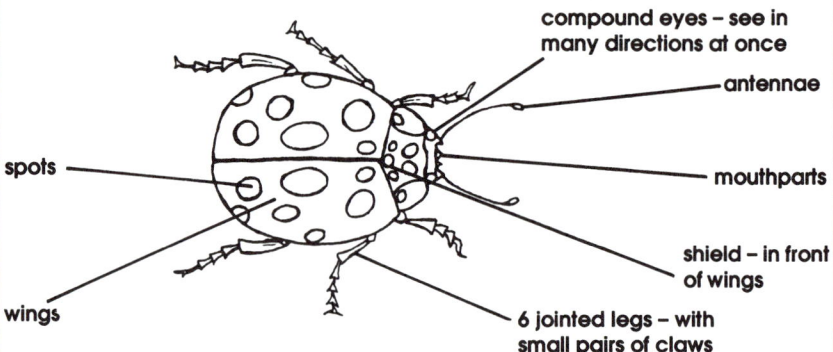

Ladybirds provide a good opportunity to observe complete metamorphosis (change of form) within weeks. They hibernate during the winter and mate during the spring and summer. The female lays batches of eggs which hatch within days. The young larvae eat, moult and change to tough-skinned pupae within a few weeks. In a further two weeks adults emerge.

Collecting and caring for ladybirds

- Ladybirds can be found from April to September. Since they feed on aphids, the children should look in areas such as around roses, lupins and thistles. A damp paint brush or piece of paper should be used to collect them and quickly transfer them to a container. A classroom home can be made from a transparent plastic container. They can be kept for one to two weeks but must be fed a supply of live aphids. Any eggs should be left on the plant where they are laid until they hatch. The larvae can be transferred to another container with a good supply of live aphids. They will need to be gently lifted on to the aphid food plant. In a warm classroom the life-cycle development will be quicker than it would be outdoors.

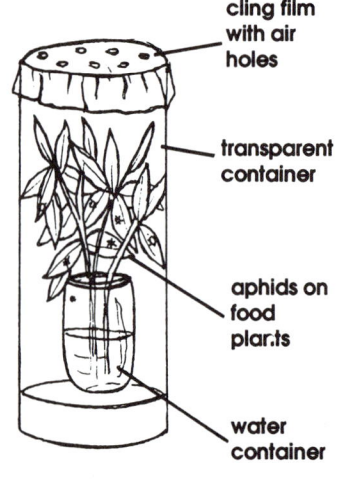
container

34   IDEAS BANK – *Minibeasts*   © Folens

A ladybird's life-cycle

- Observe the different stages of a ladybird's life.
- Use the wheel below to record what happens at each stage.
- Use the outside circle to record the dates of your observation.

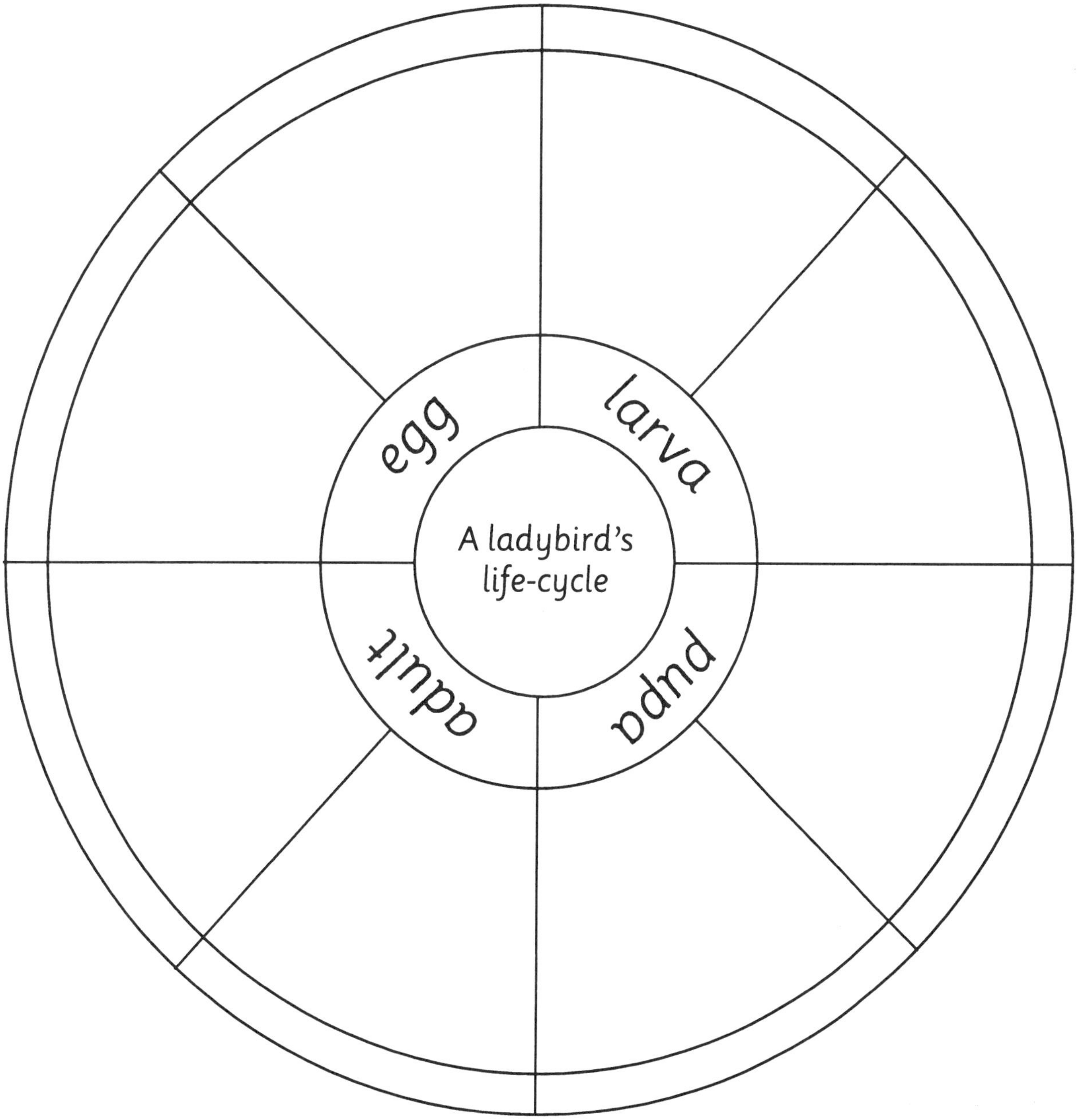

You will need:
- batches of ladybird eggs in suitable container
- aphids
- food plant
- stereo microscope
- hand lens

A ladybird's life-cycle

egg — larva — pupa — adult

- Make some models to show a ladybird's life-cycle.

 Wash your hands.

Spiders – Ideas page

Aims

- To be aware of predator-prey feeding relationships.
- To communicate detailed observations through drawings.
- To understand conditions spiders need for survival.

Activities

- First, encourage the children to observe a garden or house spider in its natural environment. Give them a data-collection chart, such as the one below:

Where does the spider wait?	
Why can't the insect escape?	
Why doesn't the spider become trapped by its own web?	
How does the spider approach its prey?	
Does the spider eat its prey immediately?	
How does the spider feed on its prey?	

- Have the children draw, label and make a habitat for the spider.
- If the children make errors on their sheet they should be pointed out before they are allowed to collect and keep a spider.

Background

Spiders are arthropods, belonging to the class Arachnida. They are predators. Having caught their prey they bite it, and the fangs squirt a poison inside it that paralyses the prey. The spider does not eat its victim immediately but wraps it in silk to save for later. When it is ready to eat, juices from the spider's mouth are poured on to the prey, turning the insides into liquid that the spider sucks up. Silk is spun from spinnerets located at the rear end of a spider's abdomen. Not all webs are the same. An orb web is produced by the garden or house spider to trap flying insects. The spiral threads contain a sticky 'glue'. Spiders have oily feet to prevent them from sticking to their web.

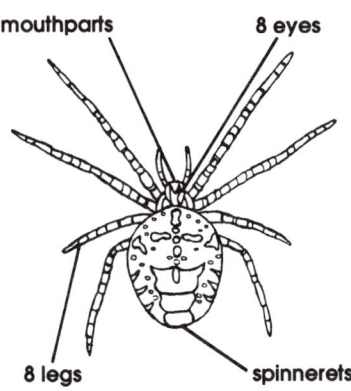

Collecting and caring for spiders

- Where you see a web you will probably find a spider. Look in damp places such as in a greenhouse, under trees and logs and inside sheds. Use a soft paintbrush to gently place the spider into a plastic container. Do not put two spiders into the same container. One might eat the other!

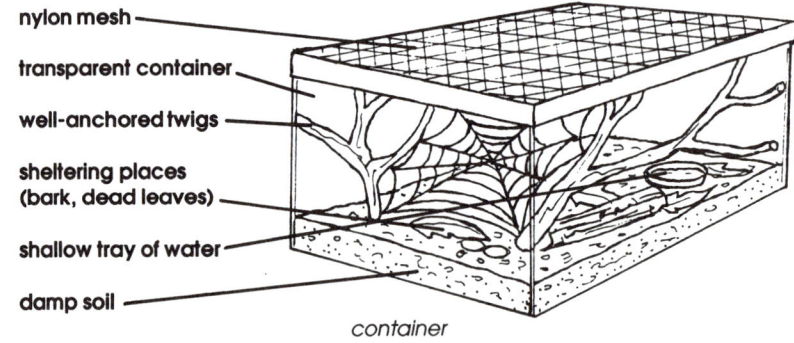

container

- Keep the spider's home damp and away from heat and direct sunlight. A spider's diet in the wild is live animals, but it can be kept in captivity for one week without food provided it has water to drink.

Development

- Make detailed observational drawings of the web spinning process.
- Investigate what happens when two spiders have their webs exchanged.
- Find out whether a spider's second web is identical to its first.
- Investigate whether varying the amount of 'supports' alters the structure of the web.
- Find out what happens if the position of a web is changed, for example turned upside down.

Spider watch

You will need:
- transparent container
- nylon mesh
- string
- damp soil
- twigs (with and without leaves)
- bark
- dead leaves
- shallow tray of water

- In the tank below, draw and label the habitat that a spider needs.

NOW
- Make a habitat for a spider.
- Place a spider inside it and observe it spinning a web.
- Make accurate drawings of the different stages.
- How could you investigate the stickiness of the web? Are all the threads sticky?

⚠ Wash your hands.

Centipedes – Ideas page

Aims

- To develop understanding of sensitivity as an important life process.
- To gain understanding of varied conditions within an environment and their effects on animals.

Activities

- Make a choice chamber to find out if centipedes prefer light or dark.
- Working in groups, the children should first make their prediction.
- Ensure that the dark ends of the tubes are very dark so that there is a great contrast between the two conditions.
- Place ten centipedes in the middle of the choice chamber. Try to test both stone and soil centipedes.
- Record where the centipedes are (dark and/or light) after five minutes and so on.
- Discuss any similarities/differences and the fairness of the investigation. The first day's results could be due to chance, therefore the test is repeated to see if there is a reliable pattern.

Development

- Investigate whether centipedes prefer dry or damp conditions.
- Find out how fast a stone centipede can move.
- Observe how a stone centipede moves over different surfaces.

Background

Centipedes are arthropods belonging to the class called Chilopoda. There are over 40 different kinds of centipedes in Britain and several thousands throughout the world. All have flattened segmented bodies and a pair of jointed legs on each body segment. Centipedes are nocturnal, eating and moving around at night. 'Centipede' means '100 feet'. The children can count to see if their centipedes have 100 feet each. Most will not.

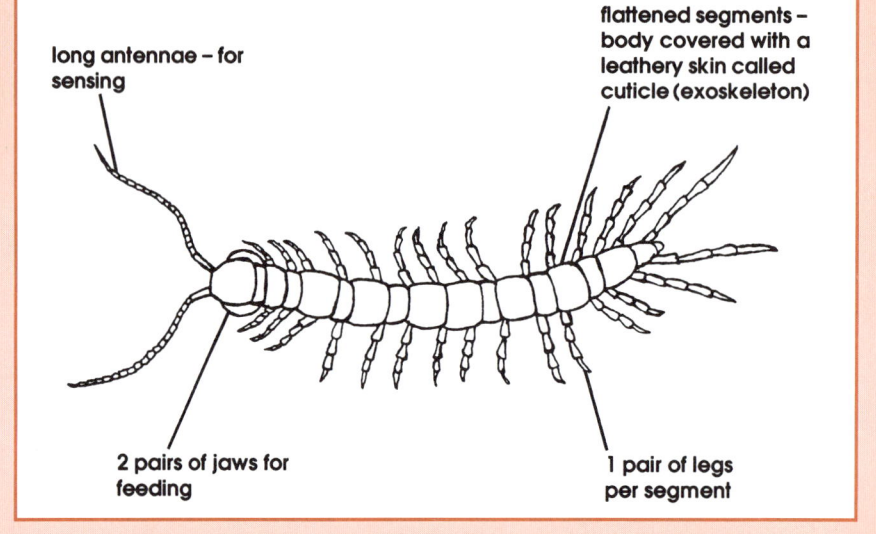

- long antennae – for sensing
- flattened segments – body covered with a leathery skin called cuticle (exoskeleton)
- 2 pairs of jaws for feeding
- 1 pair of legs per segment

Collecting and caring for centipedes

- Centipedes are fast moving but can be easily found under stones or wood in damp, earthy places or by digging in some loose earth. The children are likely to find two types – stone centipedes and soil centipedes. They should use a small plastic cup, not their fingers, to scoop them up. A centipede's movement can be slowed down, making it easier to observe, by placing it in a refrigerator for a few minutes.
- Centipedes can be kept in a plastic container half-filled with damp earth, with some stones, wood and dead leaves on top. Use cling film, with several air holes, to cover the container. Centipedes are carnivorous and will eat other minibeasts. They need to be fed minute pieces of raw meat. They can be kept for two days without food.

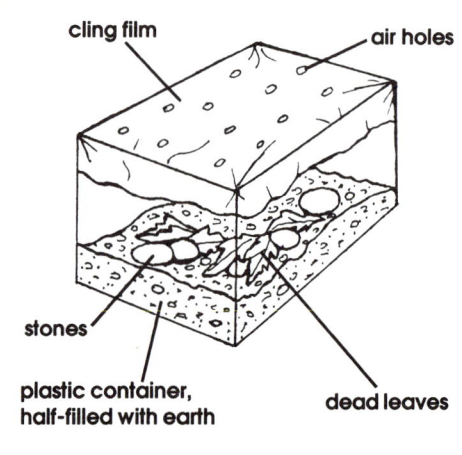

cling film, air holes, stones, plastic container, half-filled with earth, dead leaves

container

Do centipedes prefer light or dark places?

You will need:
- square, shallow container
- Plasticine
- black paper
- ten centipedes

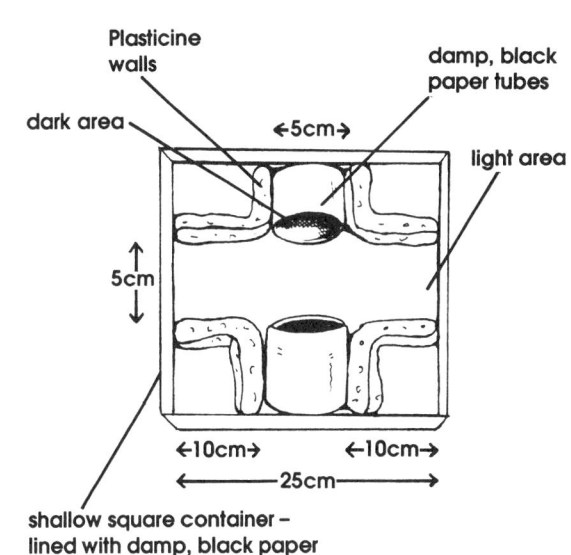

- First predict which you think centipedes prefer.
- Then make a choice chamber that has light and dark places, such as the one shown here.
- To make it fair keep the surfaces, temperatures and size of the places the same and ensure that there are dark areas and light areas.
- Put the centipedes in the middle.
- Record your findings on the charts below.

Diagram labels: Plasticine walls; dark area; damp, black paper tubes; 5cm; light area; 5cm; 10cm; 10cm; 25cm; shallow square container – lined with damp, black paper

Day 1

after mins	dark	light
5		
10		
15		
20		
25		
30		

Day 2

after mins	dark	light
5		
10		
15		
20		
25		
30		

Day 3

after mins	dark	light
5		
10		
15		
20		
25		
30		

NOW
- What did you discover? Was your prediction right?
- How did you make sure that your test was fair?
- Why was the test repeated?

⚠ Wash your hands.

Millipedes – Ideas page

Aims

- To develop understanding of the life processes of movement, nutrition and sensitivity.
- To develop the scientific skills of observing and planning experimental work.

Background

Millipedes are arthropods belonging to the class known as Diplopoda, meaning 'double-footed'. Over 7000 different species of millipedes have been found around the world. All millipedes have two pairs of short legs on most of their body segments. (This is one way of distinguishing them from centipedes.) Millipedes are very useful in breaking down organic matter and thus forming fertile soil. They are herbivorous, eating fruits, vegetables, leaves and twigs. When in danger millipedes exude a foul-smelling liquid, so the children need to wash their hands after handling them.

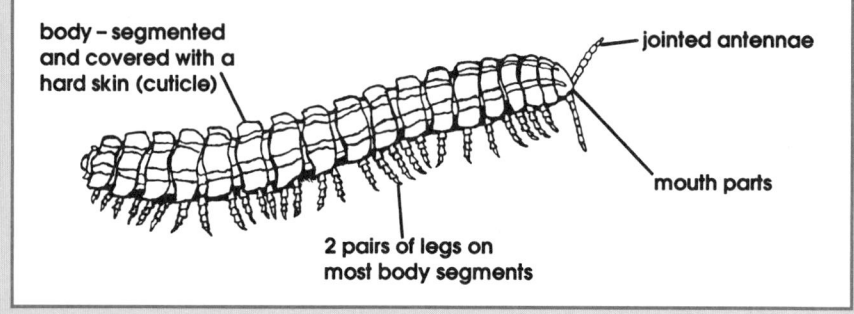

- body – segmented and covered with a hard skin (cuticle)
- jointed antennae
- mouth parts
- 2 pairs of legs on most body segments

Activities

- The activity sheet should be used to aid the children as they observe how a millipede moves and behaves.

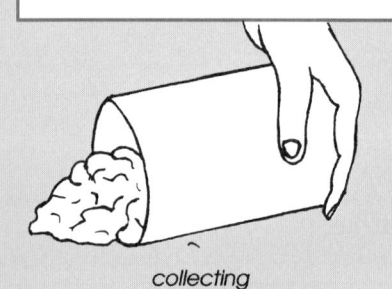

collecting

Collecting and caring for millipedes

- Millipedes are slow moving and often inactive during the day. They can be found in vegetable gardens, around rotting leaves and under bark, bricks and stones. They can be attracted by placing grapefruit halves in these places for them to crawl into. A plastic cup can be used to scoop them up (along with soil) before placing them into a small plastic container.
- A millipede 'home' can be made from a large plastic container covered in cling film with air holes. It should contain earth, dead leaves and stones. Millipedes are easily dehydrated and so damp and dry areas need to be created. Feed them small pieces of apple. It is probably best to keep millipedes for a maximum of two days before returning them to their natural habitat.

Development

- Find out if millipedes can smell. The children will need some strong smelling things. Remind them to devise a fair test.
- Find out which foods millipedes prefer.
- Investigate the conditions millipedes prefer, for example light, dark, damp or dry.
- Do some speed tests with millipedes.
- Make a book about millipedes including details of investigations carried out, photographs and drawings. The children might use a word-processor or desk-top publishing package for this.

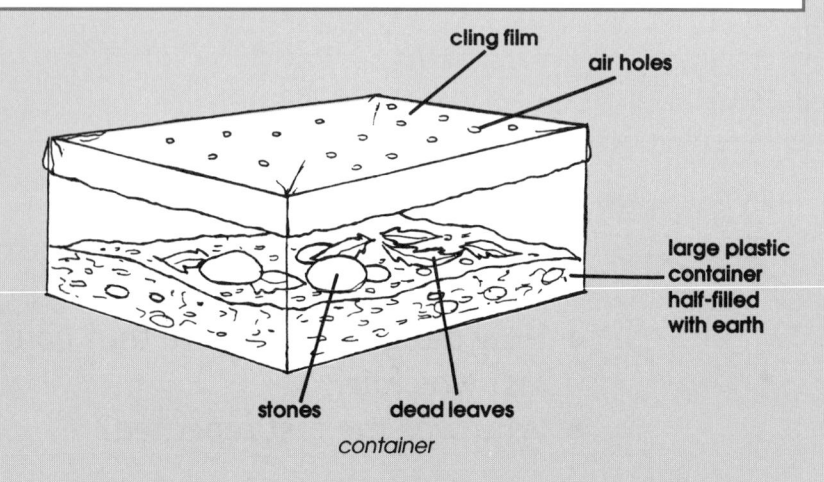

- cling film
- air holes
- large plastic container half-filled with earth
- stones
- dead leaves

container

Make a millipede book

You will need:
- A3 paper
- pencil
- scissors
- Perspex sheet
- glue
- sand
- millipedes
- hand lens

- Ask your teacher to help you make a concertina book. Cut out the two pages below and stick them on to the first two pages of your book.

⚠ Wash your hands.

- On page 1 draw and label a millipede.
- On page 2 draw and label some diagrams to show how it moves.
- Write about what happens when sand or earth or stones and gravel are put around your millipede.
- Find out how fast a millipede moves. Do they all move at the same speed? Write about your investigation in your millipede book.

Classifying minibeasts – Ideas page

Aims

- To develop an appreciation of the great variety of minibeasts within the environment.
- To develop an understanding that minibeasts have different characteristics and that these can be used for classification and identification.
- To develop the scientific skills of observation, identification and classification.

Background

Scientists use a classification system developed in the eighteenth century by a Swedish botanist, Linnaeus. He gave all animals and plants Latin names. All living things are divided into kingdoms – this includes the animal kingdom and the plant kingdom. Each kingdom is sub-divided into divisions and then into classes, orders, families and species. New animals that are discovered are given names, by an international group of scientists. Their characteristics are examined and they are assigned to a position in the classification table. The animal kingdom contains about five million species. Those animals with backbones are called vertebrates. Animals without backbones, and this includes 'minibeasts', are called invertebrates. The diagram shown below is a simplified version of the classification of the animal kingdom, showing some of the animals often met under the topic of 'minibeasts':

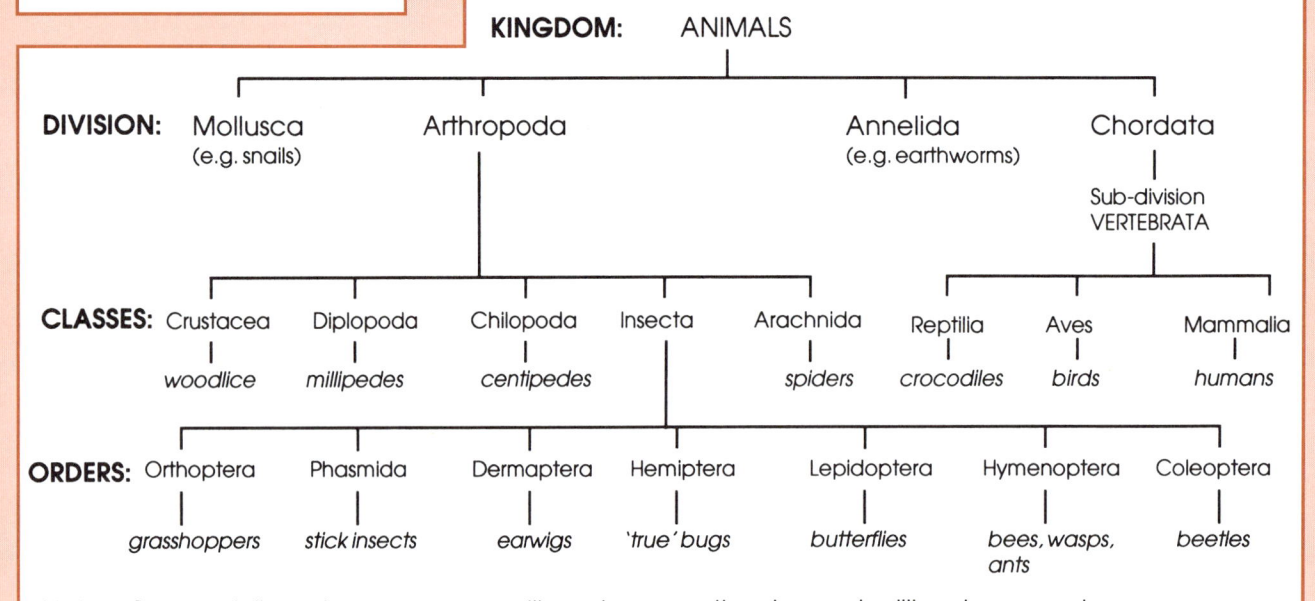

KINGDOM: ANIMALS

DIVISION: Mollusca (e.g. snails) | Arthropoda | Annelida (e.g. earthworms) | Chordata

Sub-division VERTEBRATA

CLASSES: Crustacea (woodlice) | Diplopoda (millipedes) | Chilopoda (centipedes) | Insecta | Arachnida (spiders) | Reptilia (crocodiles) | Aves (birds) | Mammalia (humans)

ORDERS: Orthoptera (grasshoppers) | Phasmida (stick insects) | Dermaptera (earwigs) | Hemiptera ('true' bugs) | Lepidoptera (butterflies) | Hymenoptera (bees, wasps, ants) | Coleoptera (beetles)

Note – Some minibeasts – worms, woodlice, slugs, centipedes and millipedes – can become dehydrated and should be observed for a maximum of 15 minutes. Other creatures can be observed for up to 30 minutes before being returned to their natural environment.
Safety – Ensure that the children wash their hands after handling minibeasts.

Activities

- Explain to the children how the activity sheet works. Using it they can compare two minibeasts and list the differences between them. They should work in pairs and their observations should lead to a list of differences.
- The final part of the activity sheet suggests that the children sort minibeasts by observable features using a simple key that they have devised. To enable them to do this, provide information books with other more complicated identification keys.

Development

- The children could construct their own branching keys on a computer.

Classifying minibeasts

You will need:
- two minibeasts
- two transparent containers
- magnifier

Put two different minibeasts into two small transparent containers. Use a magnifier to observe them closely. Talk to a partner about the differences between them.

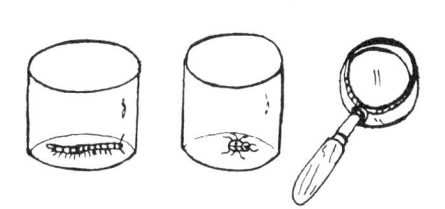

- Use this branching key to identify the two minibeasts:

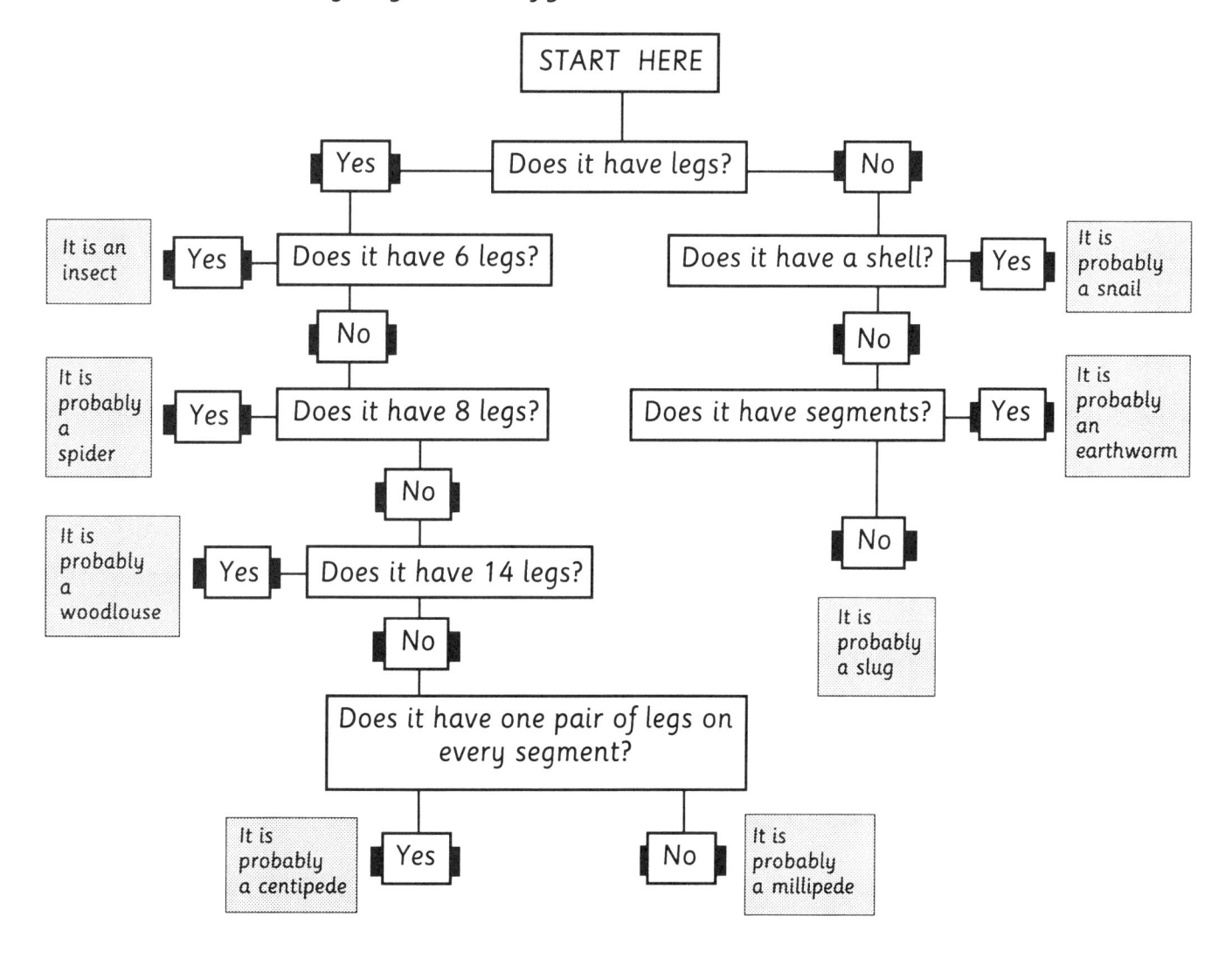

START HERE

Does it have legs?
- Yes → Does it have 6 legs?
  - Yes → It is an insect
  - No → Does it have 8 legs?
    - Yes → It is probably a spider
    - No → Does it have 14 legs?
      - Yes → It is probably a woodlouse
      - No → Does it have one pair of legs on every segment?
        - Yes → It is probably a centipede
        - No → It is probably a millipede
- No → Does it have a shell?
  - Yes → It is probably a snail
  - No → Does it have segments?
    - Yes → It is probably an earthworm
    - No → It is probably a slug

NOW
- Use information books to check the identification of your creature. Make up your own identification key for other minibeasts.

⚠ Wash your hands.

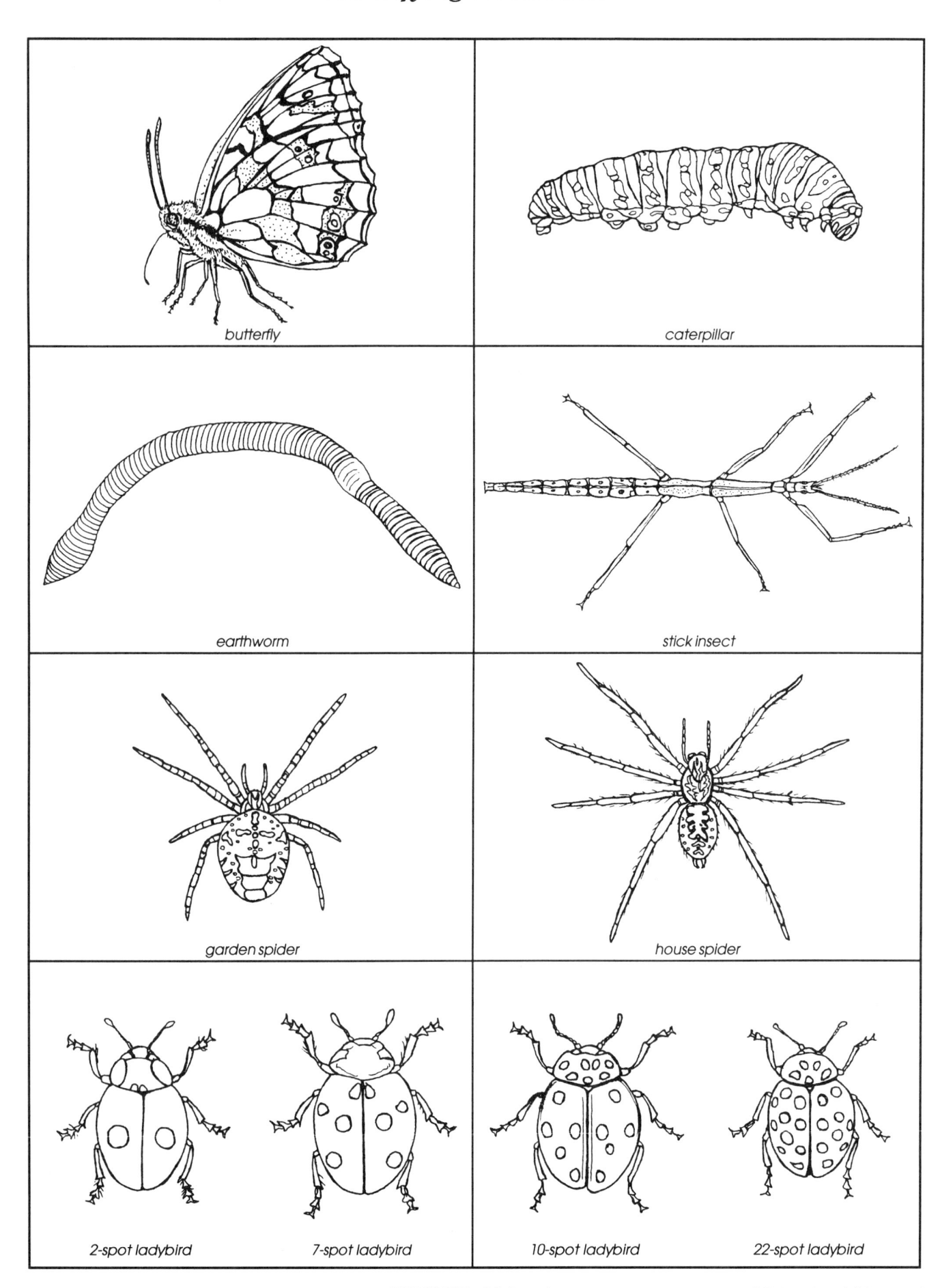

Identifying minibeasts

butterfly	caterpillar
earthworm	stick insect
garden spider	house spider
2-spot ladybird 7-spot ladybird	10-spot ladybird 22-spot ladybird

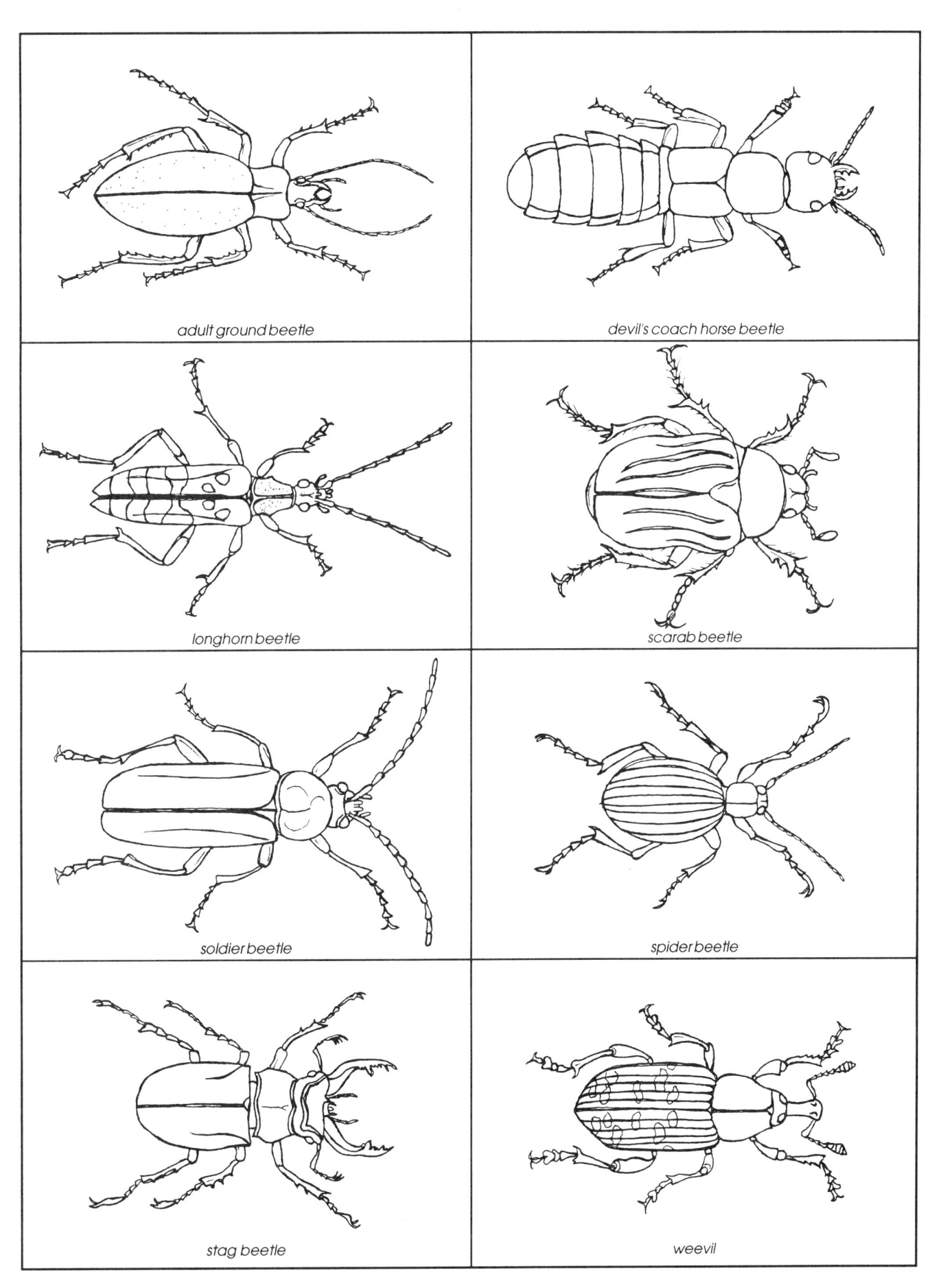

Identifying minibeasts

adult ground beetle	devil's coach horse beetle
longhorn beetle	scarab beetle
soldier beetle	spider beetle
stag beetle	weevil

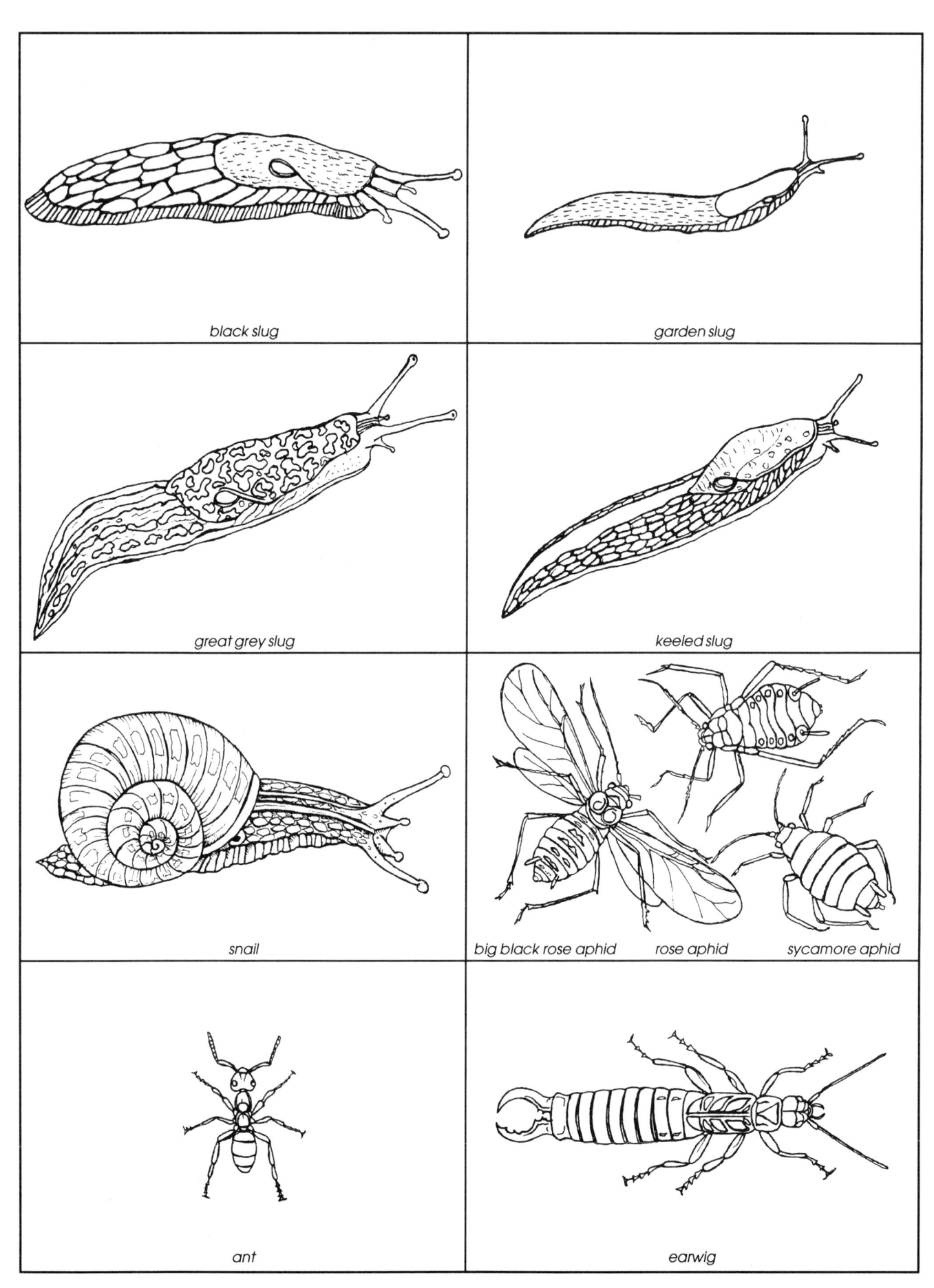

Identifying minibeasts

black slug	garden slug
great grey slug	keeled slug
snail	big black rose aphid — rose aphid — sycamore aphid
ant	earwig

46   IDEAS BANK – *Minibeasts*   © Folens (copiable page)

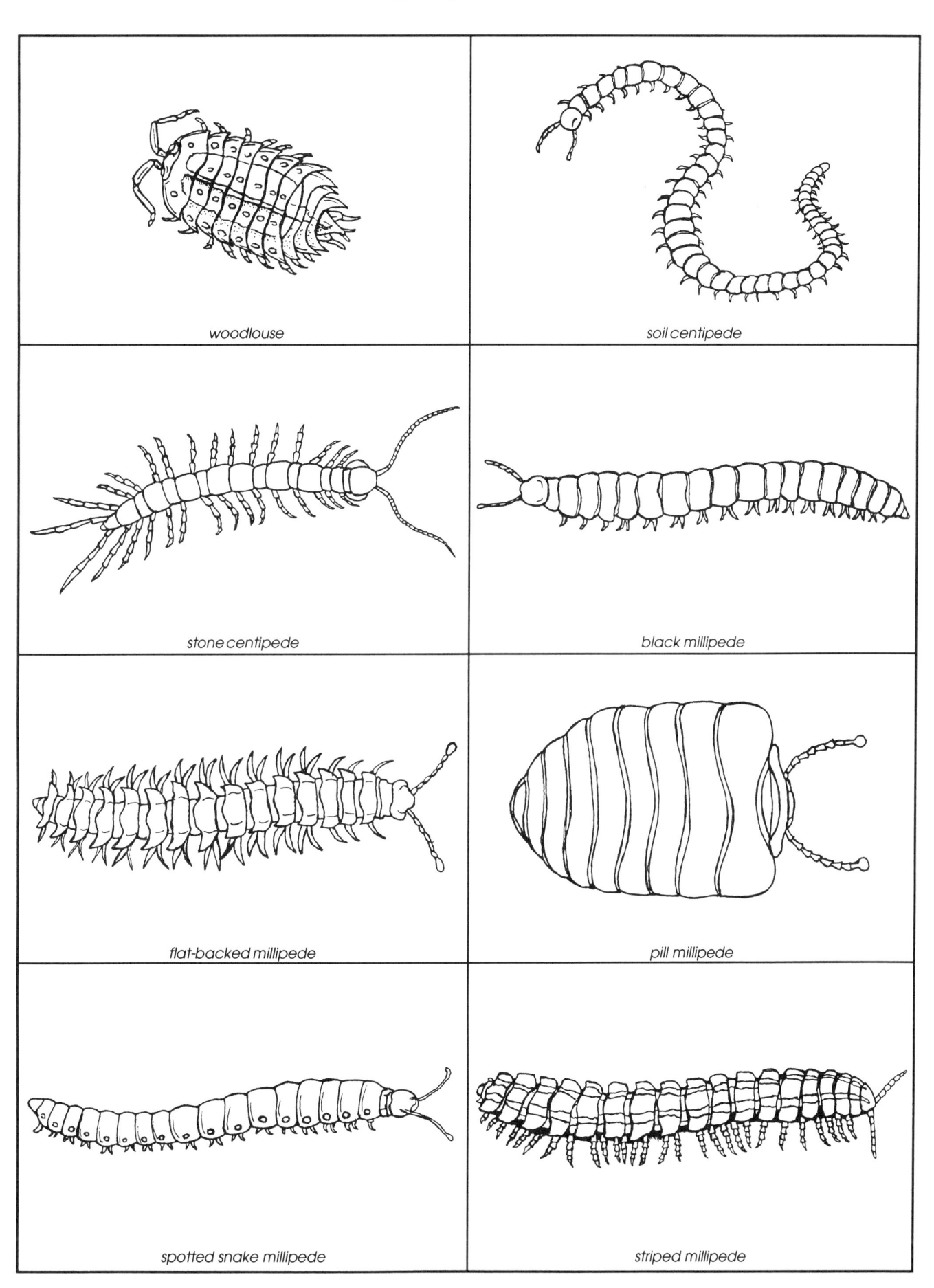

Identifying minibeasts

woodlouse	soil centipede
stone centipede	black millipede
flat-backed millipede	pill millipede
spotted snake millipede	striped millipede

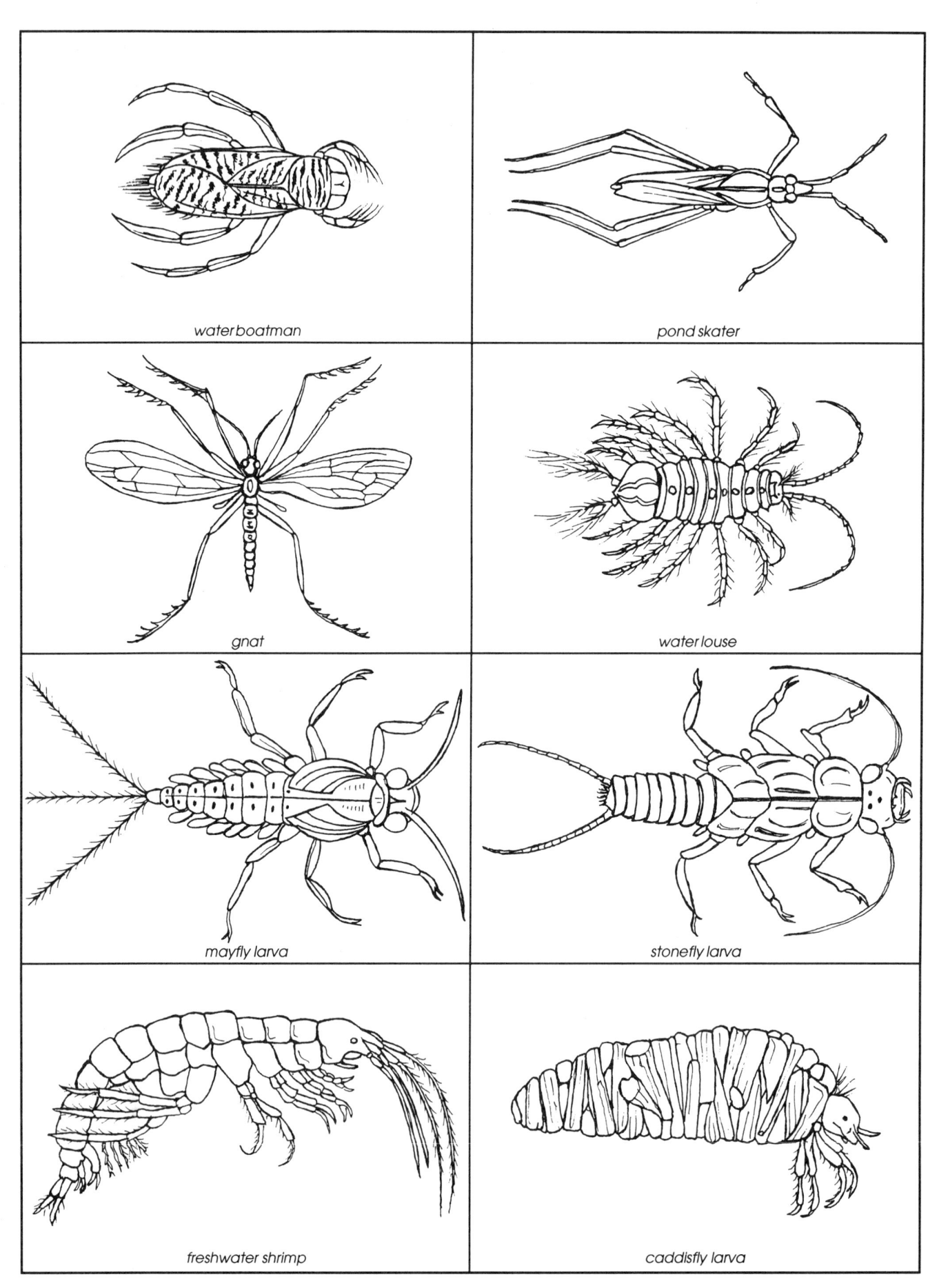

Identifying minibeasts

water boatman

pond skater

gnat

water louse

mayfly larva

stonefly larva

freshwater shrimp

caddisfly larva